Buildings

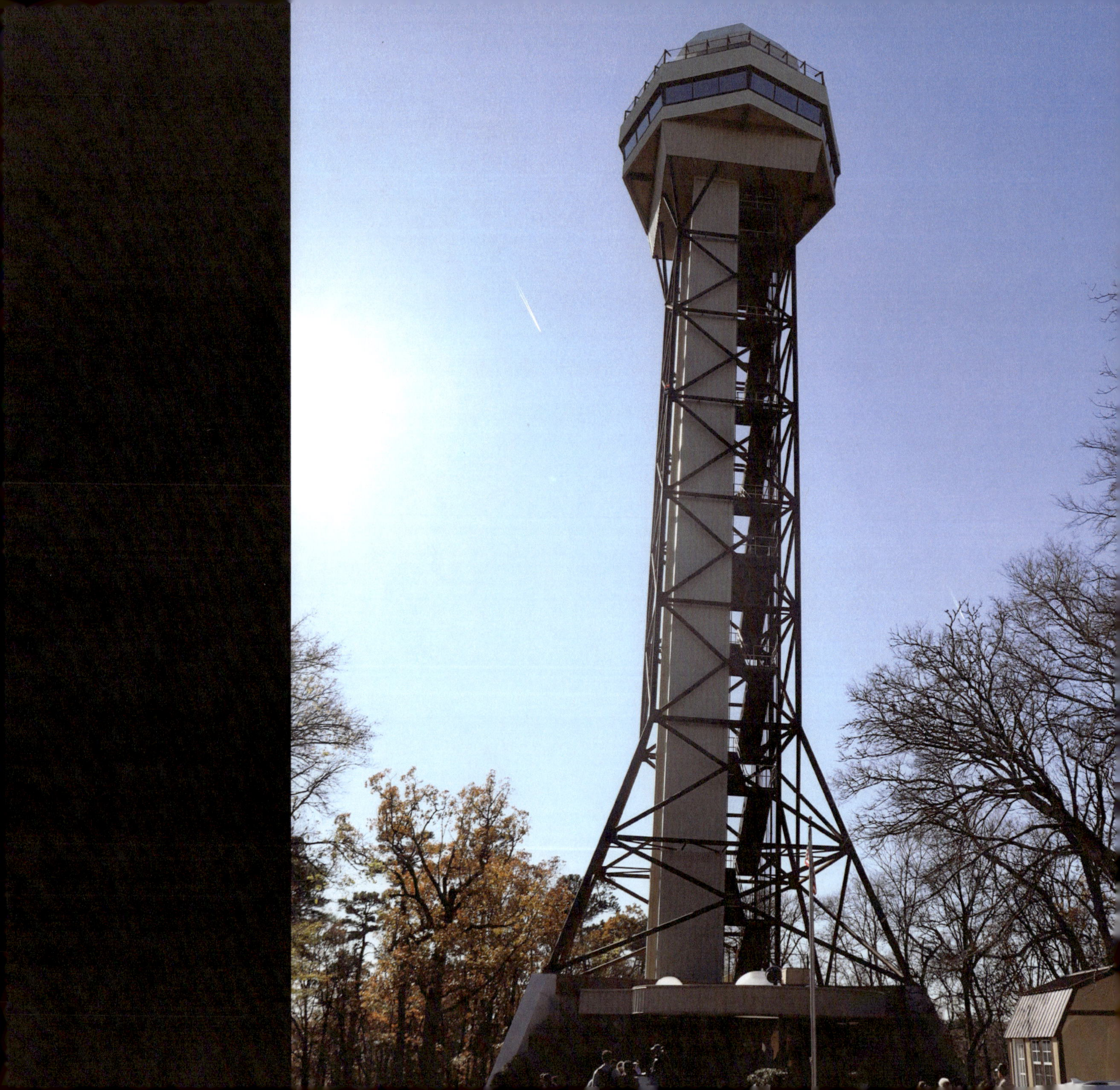

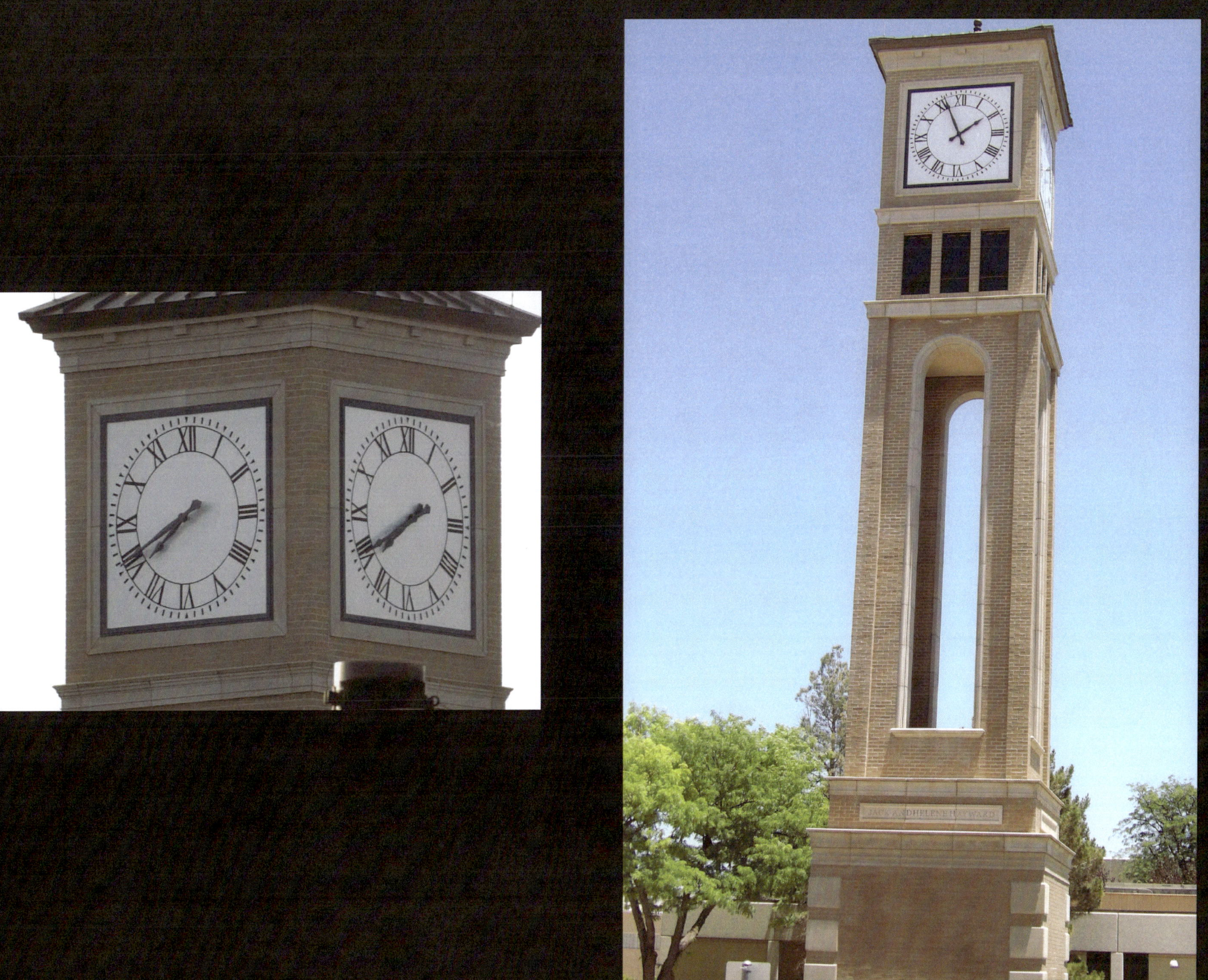

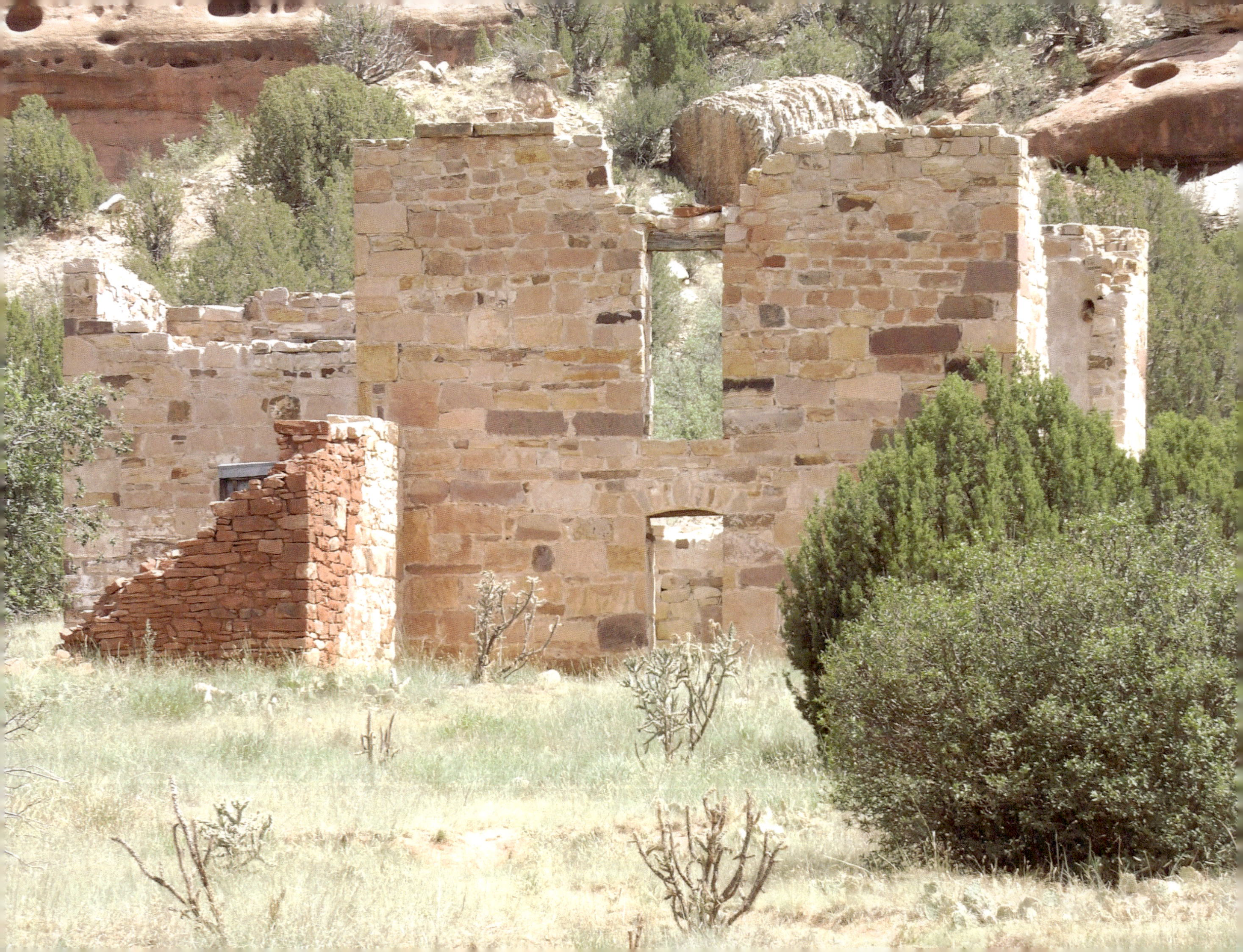

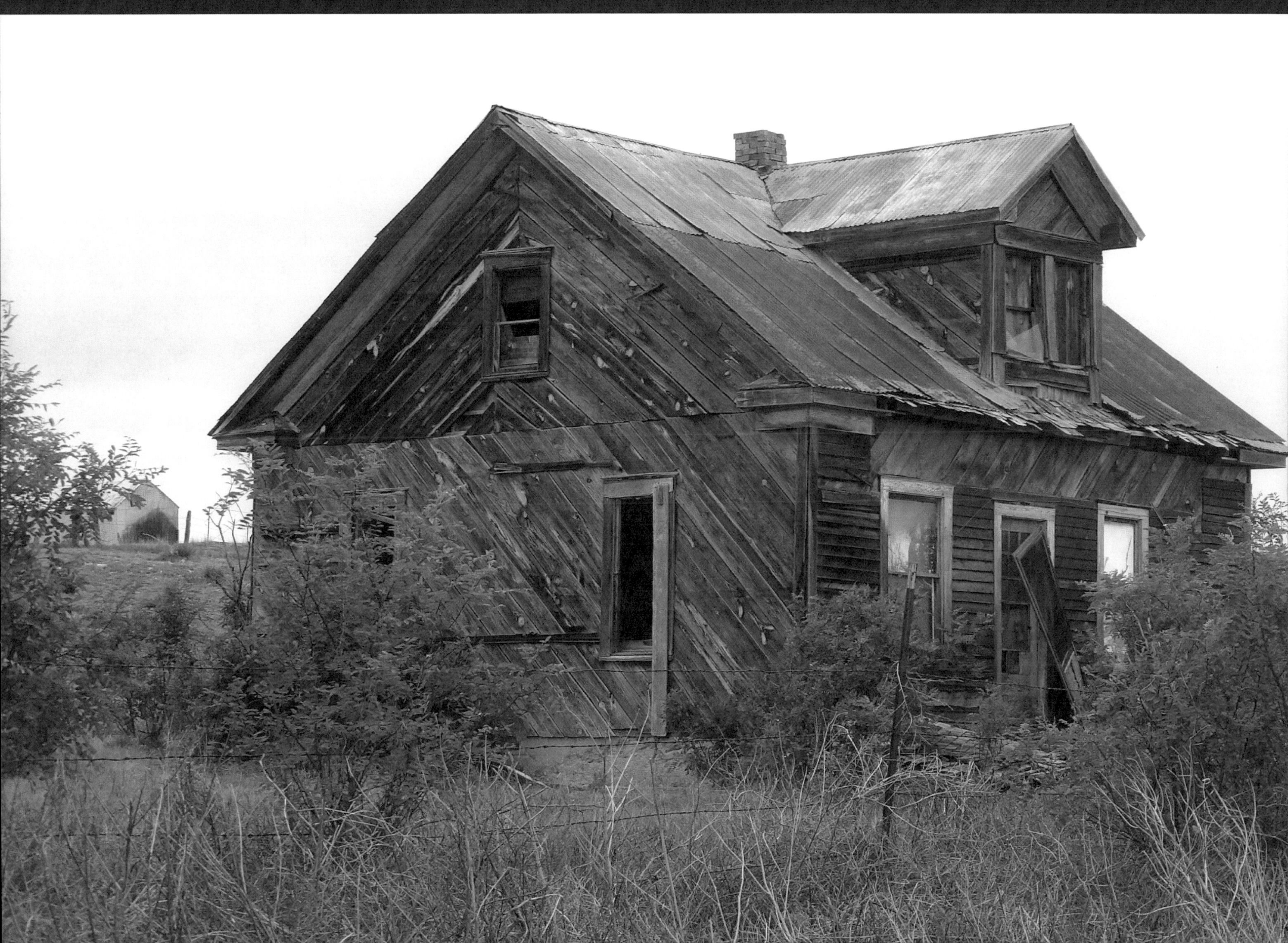

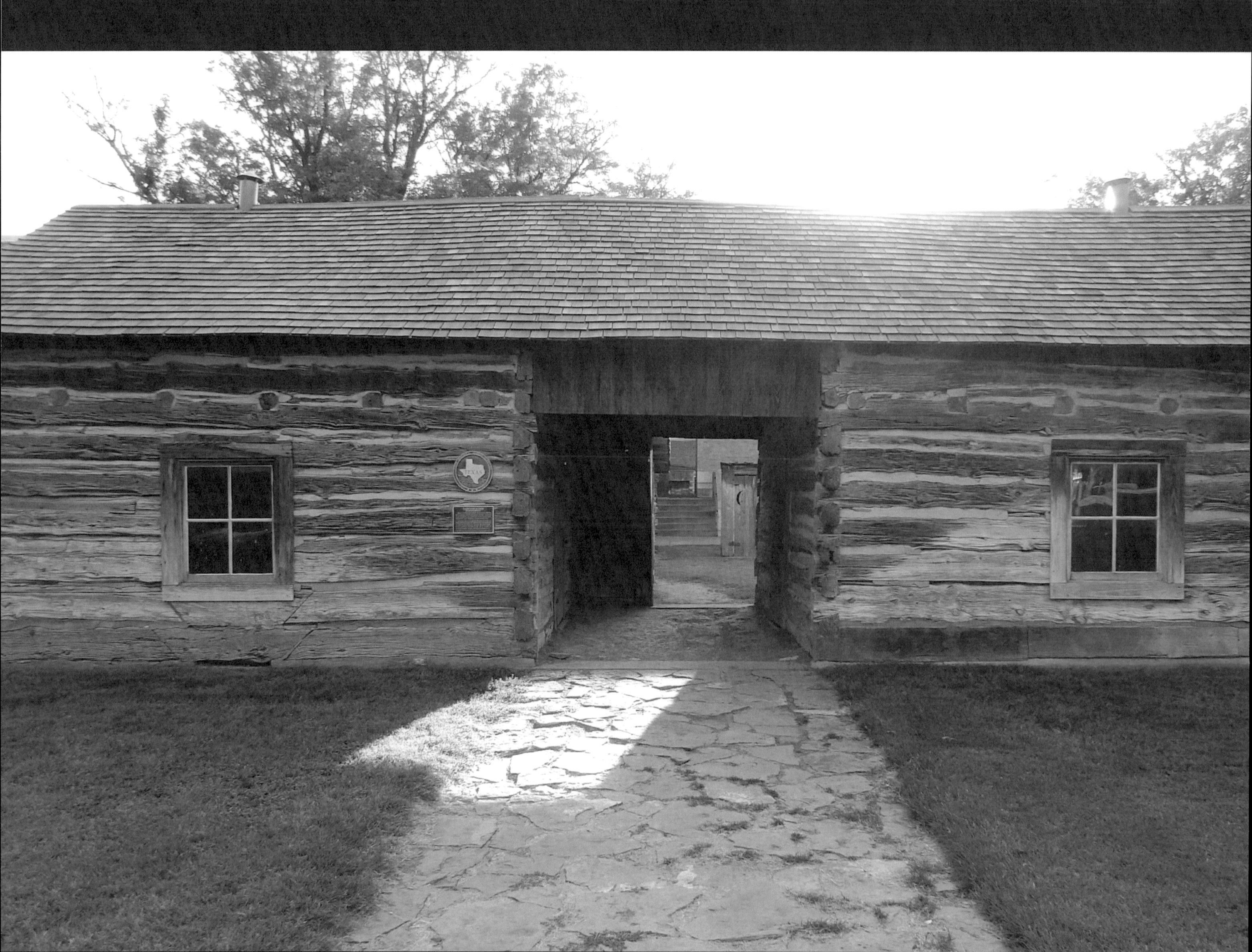

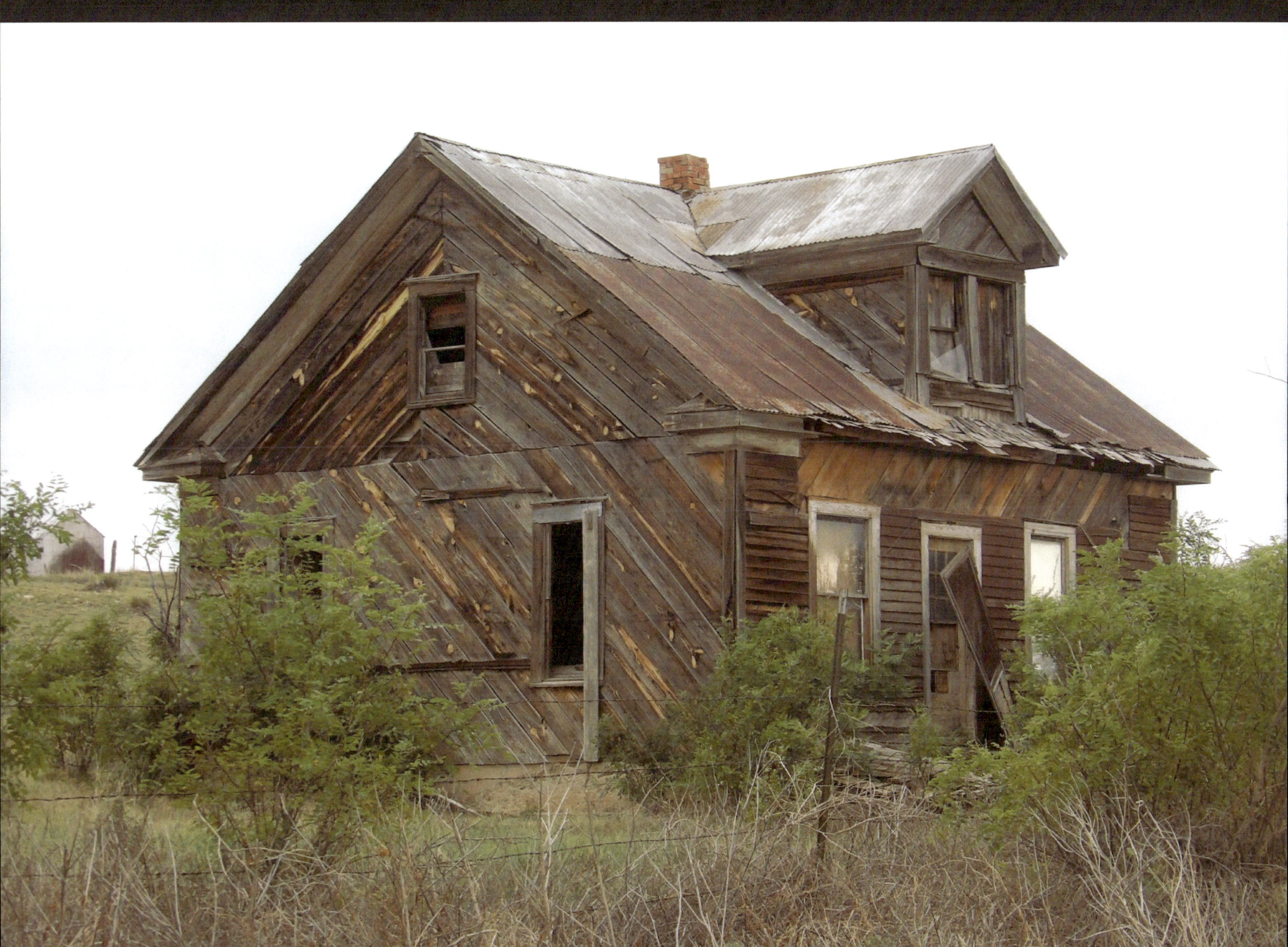

Flowers

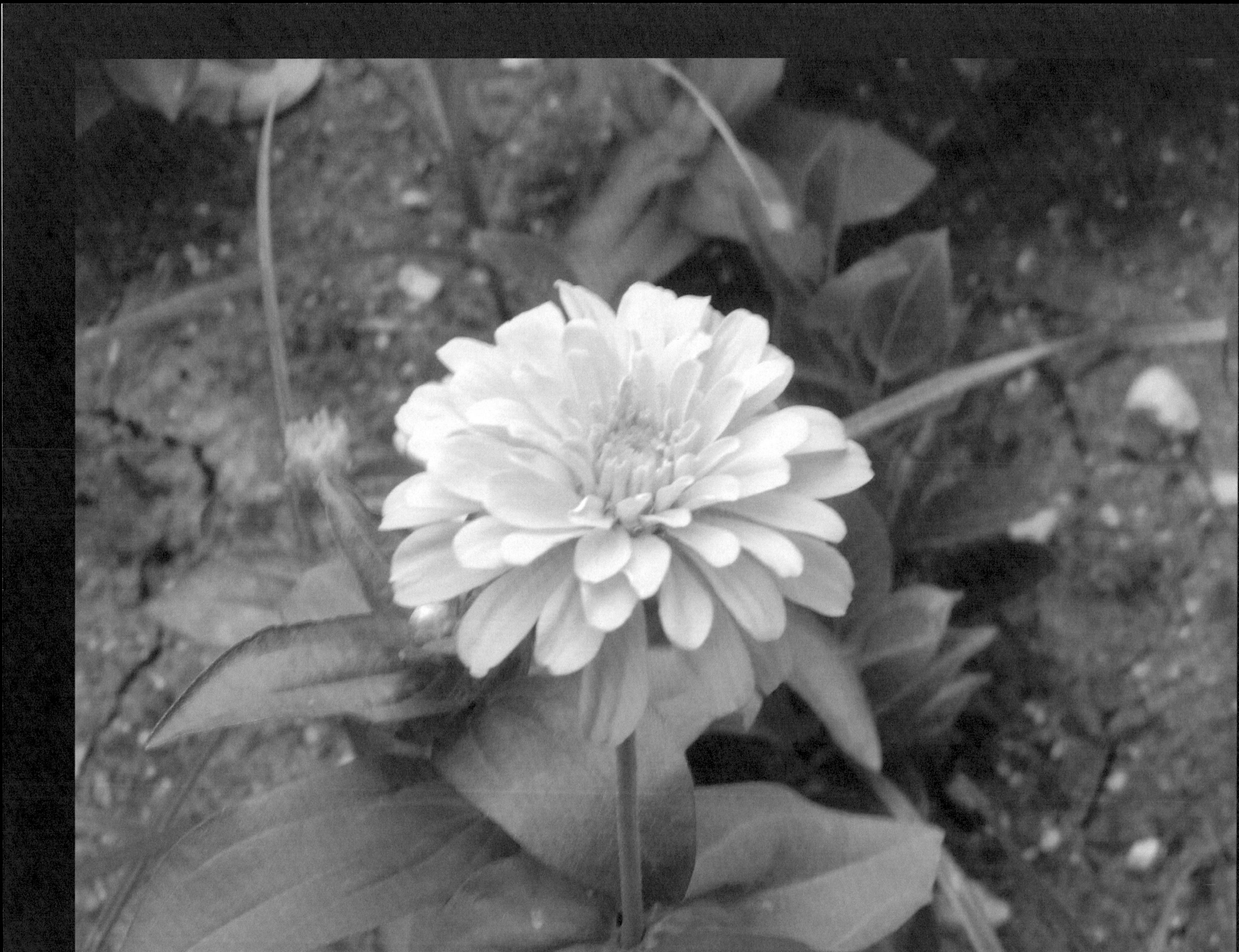

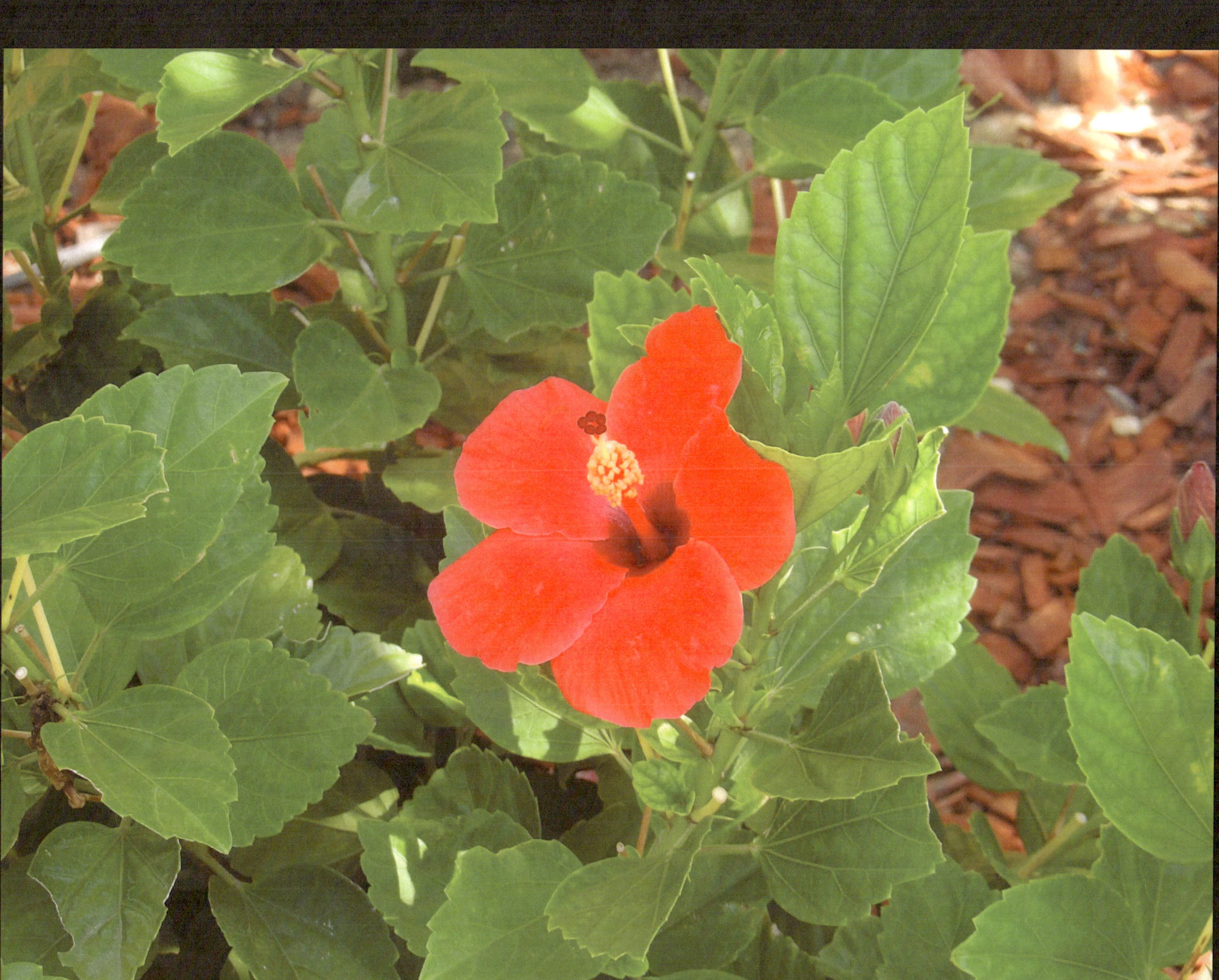

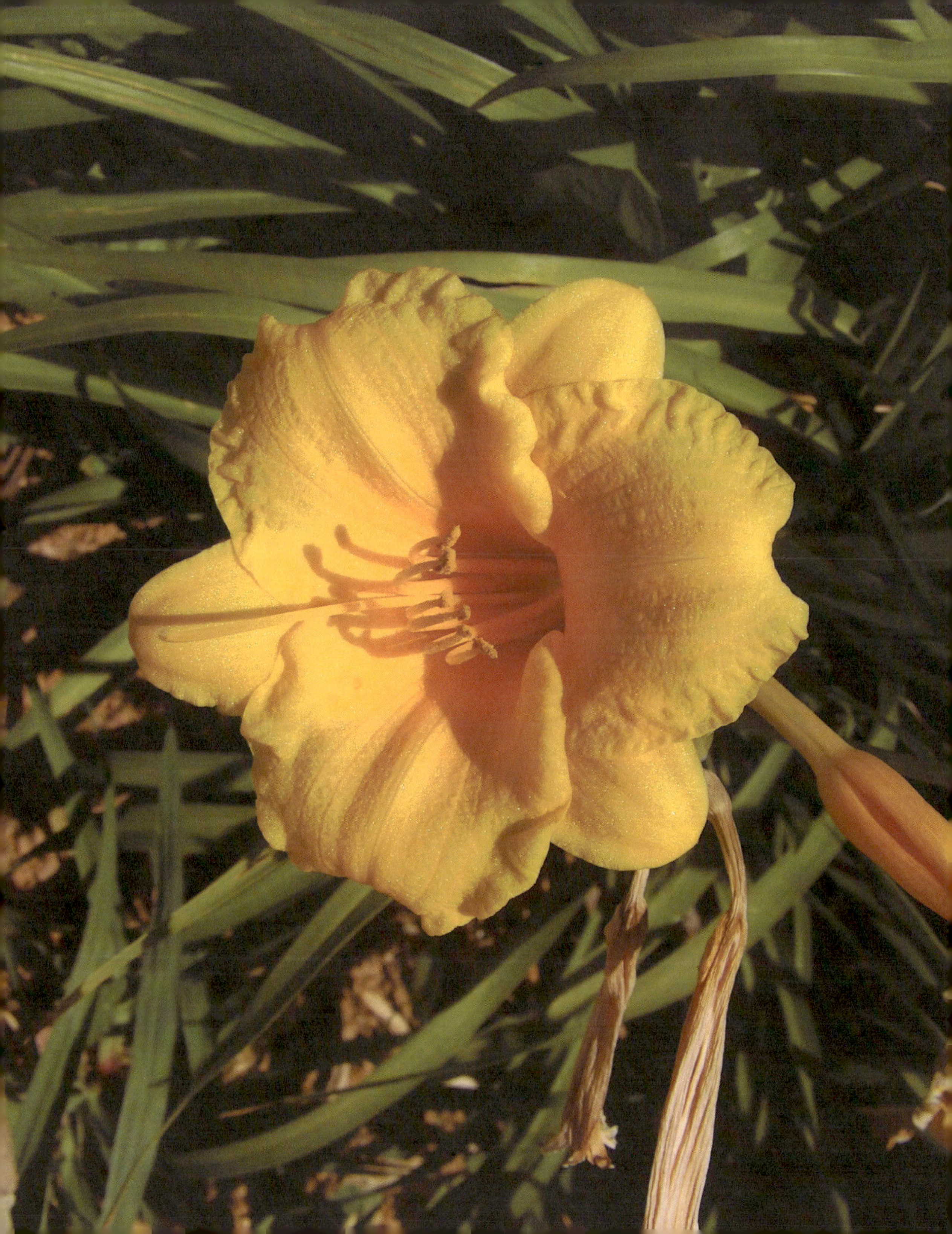

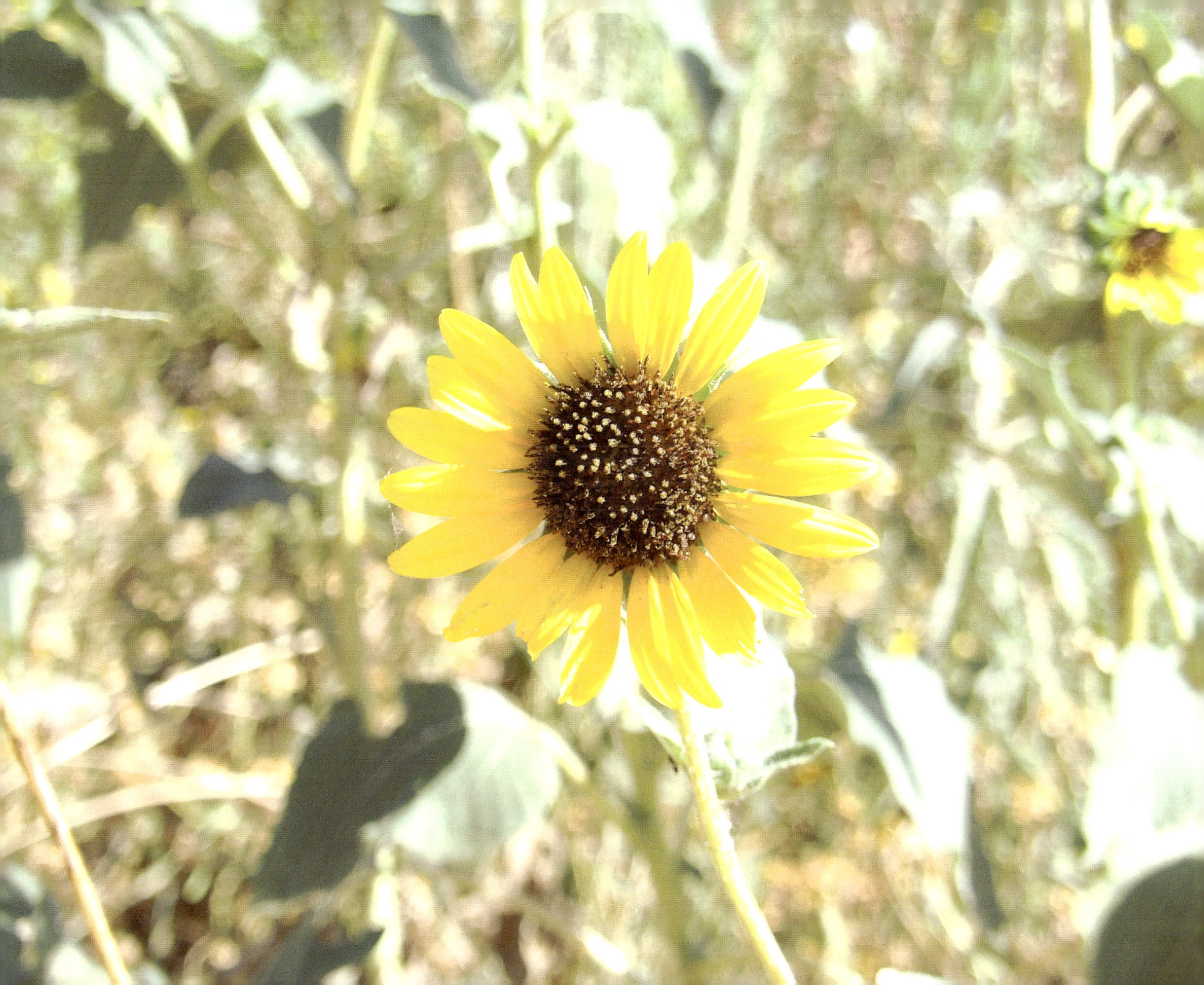

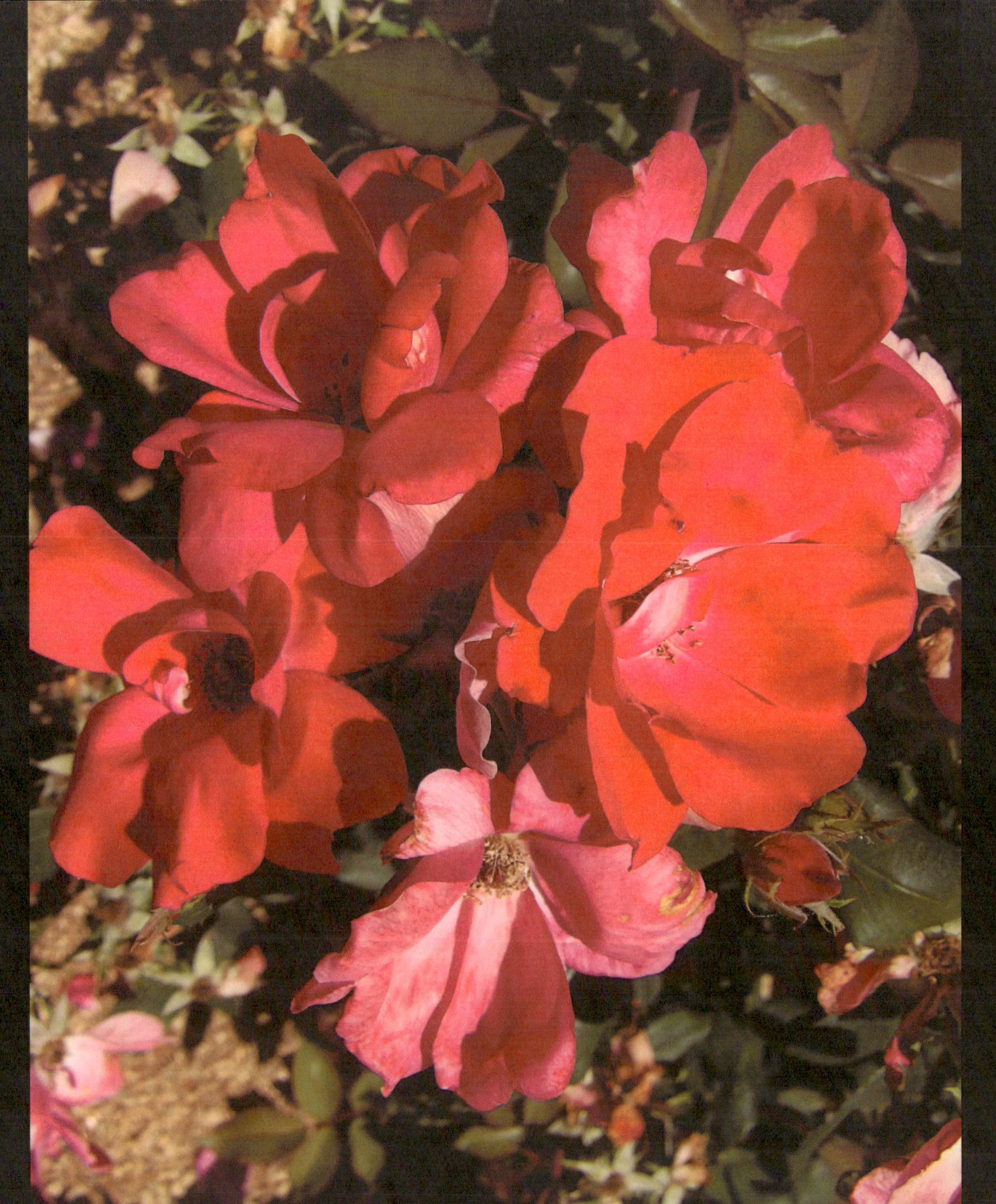

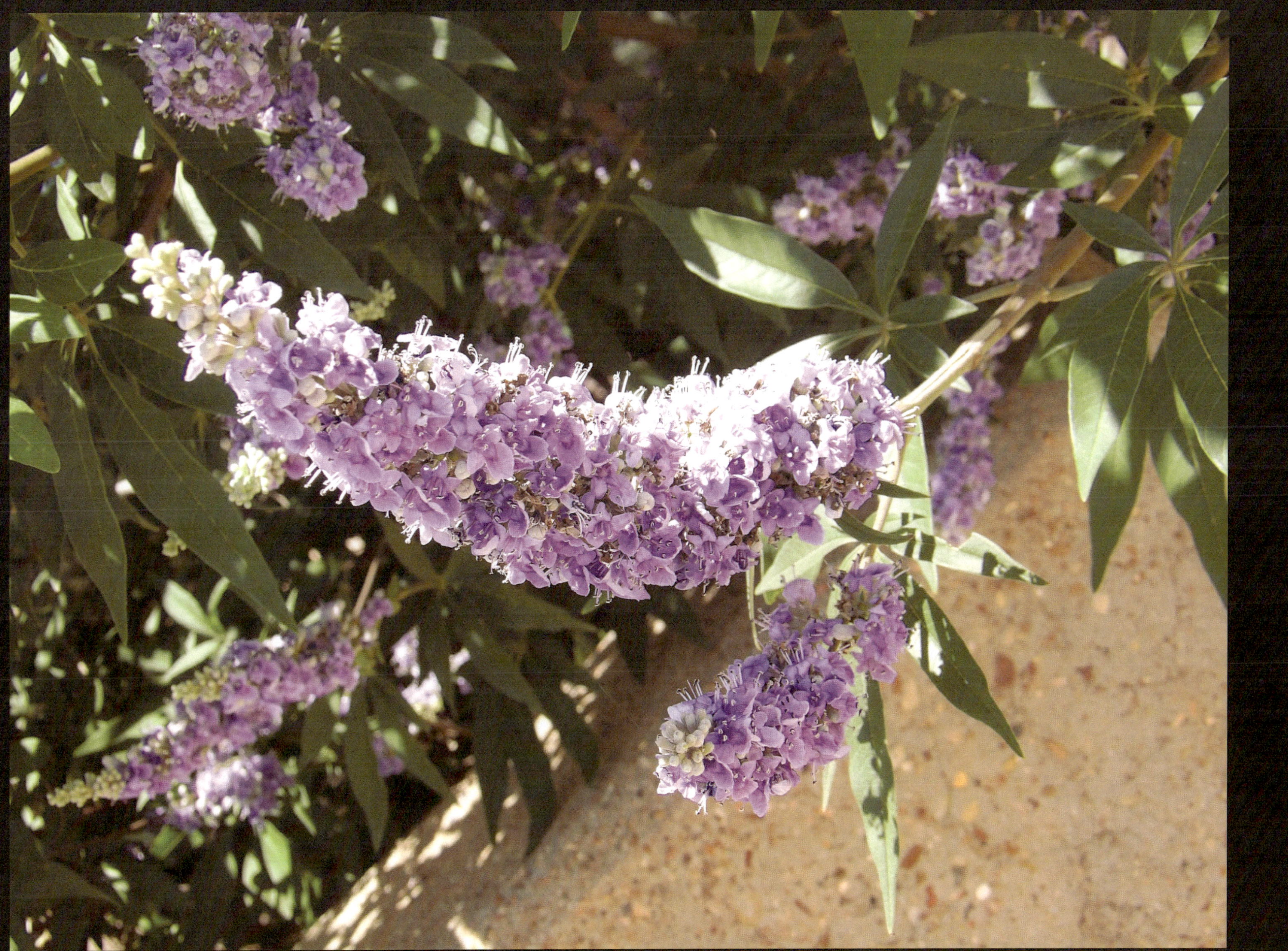

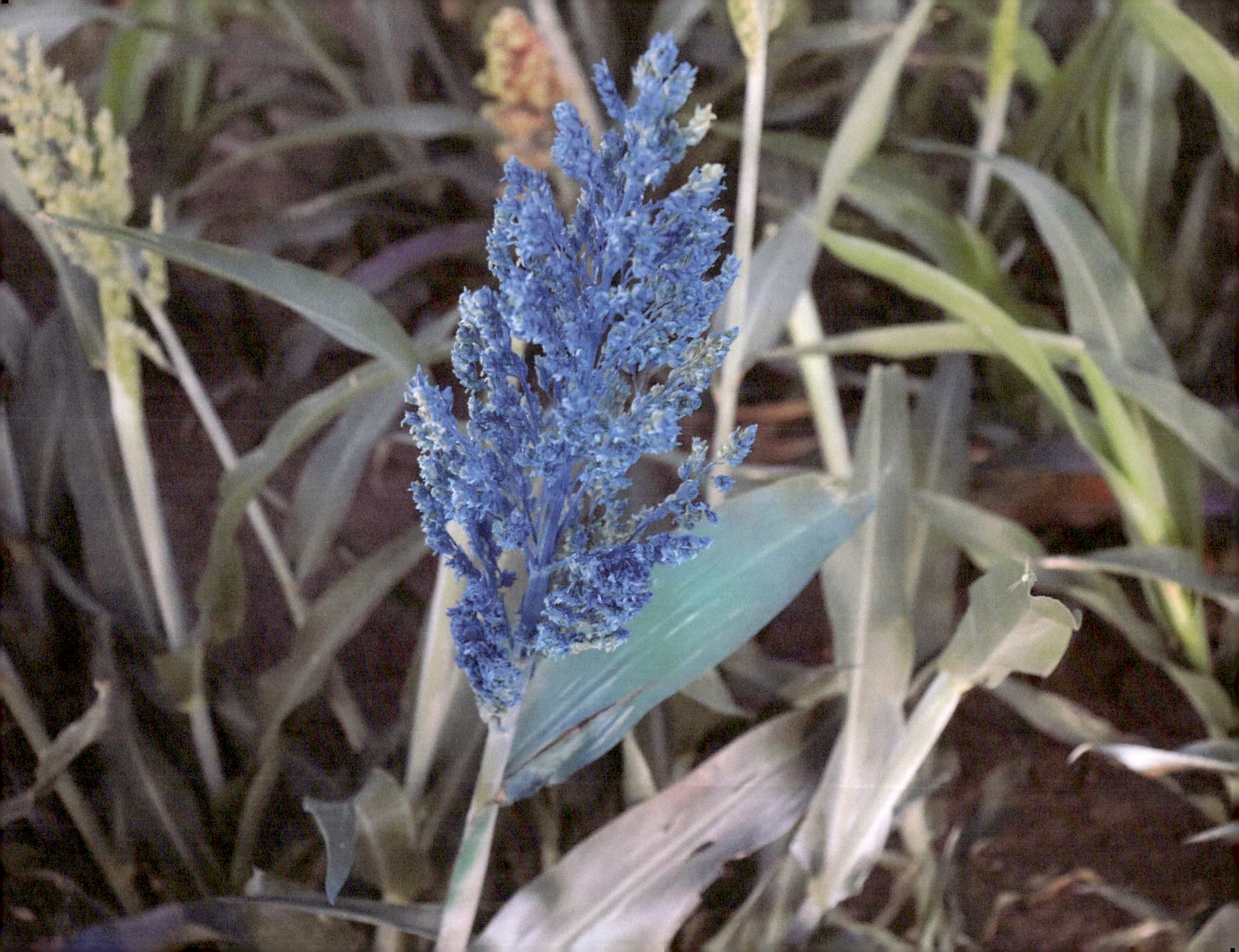

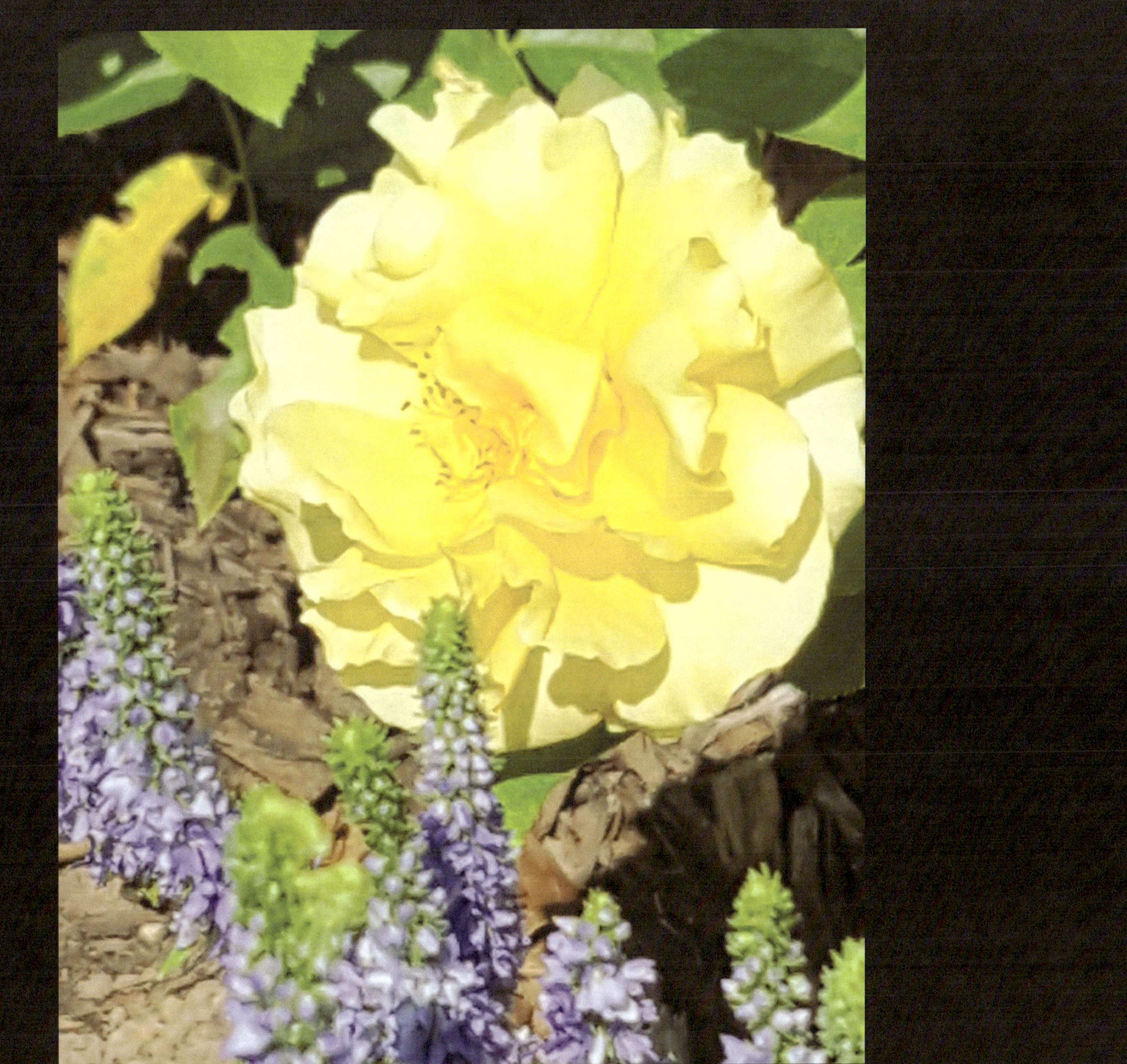

Random

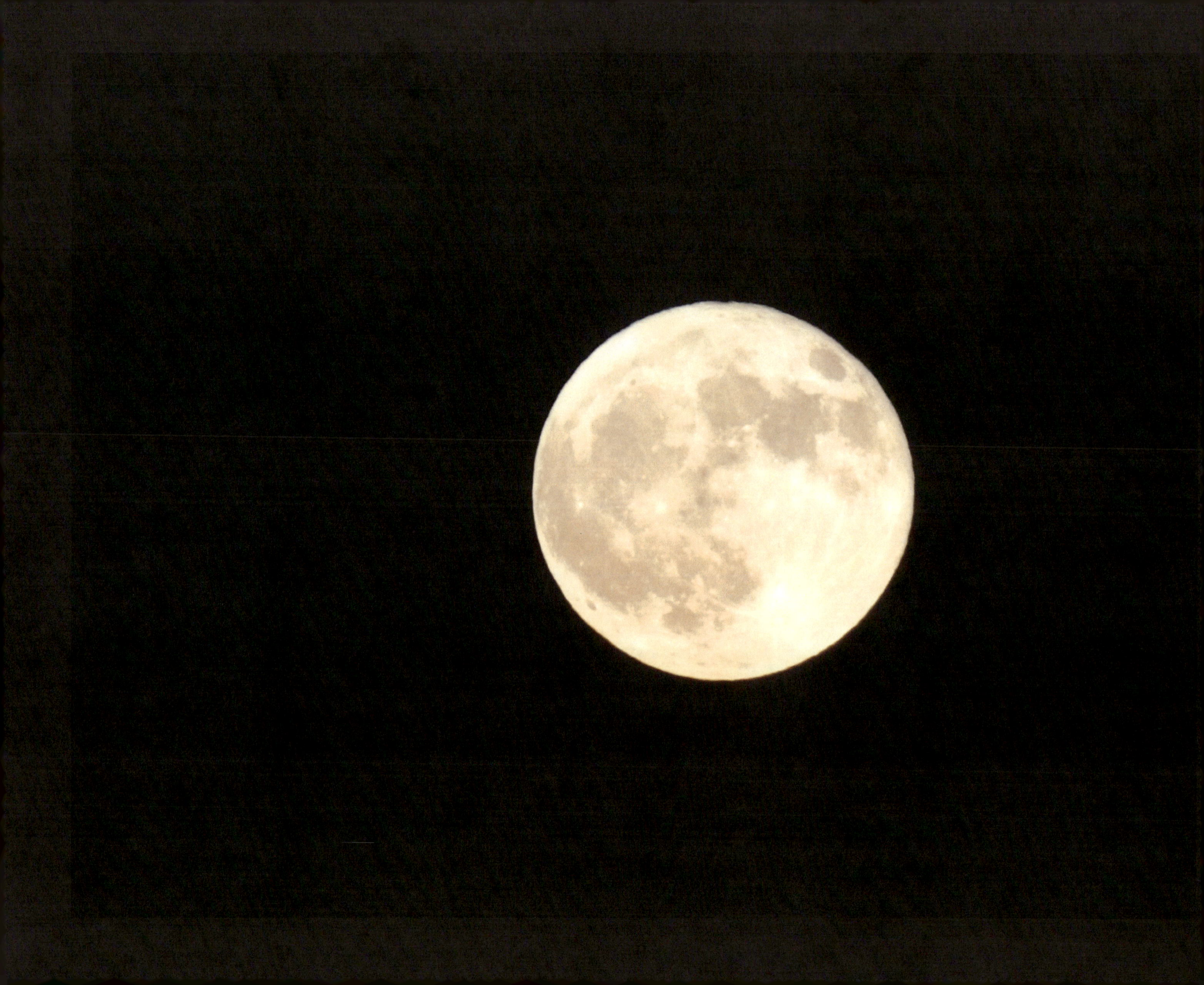

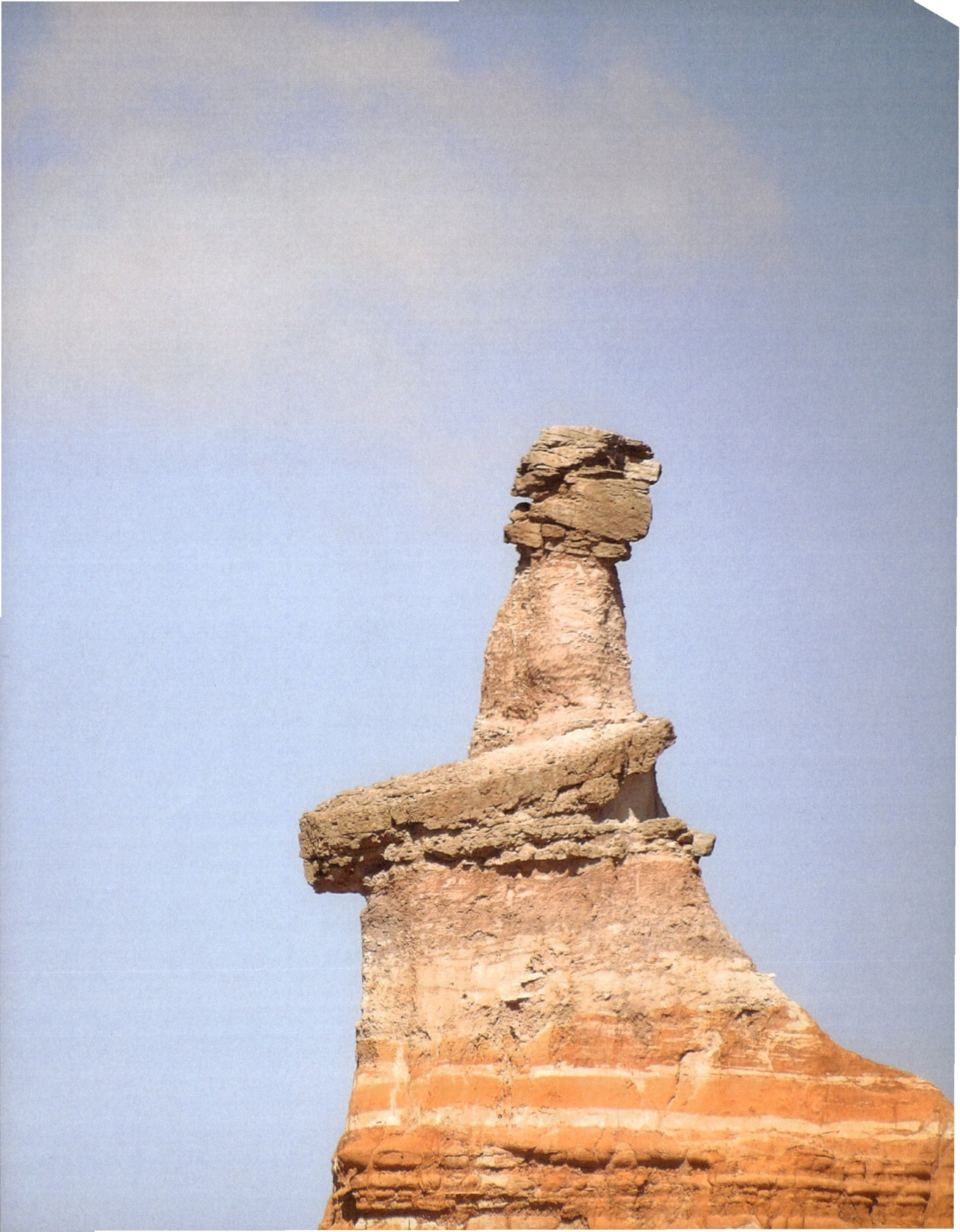

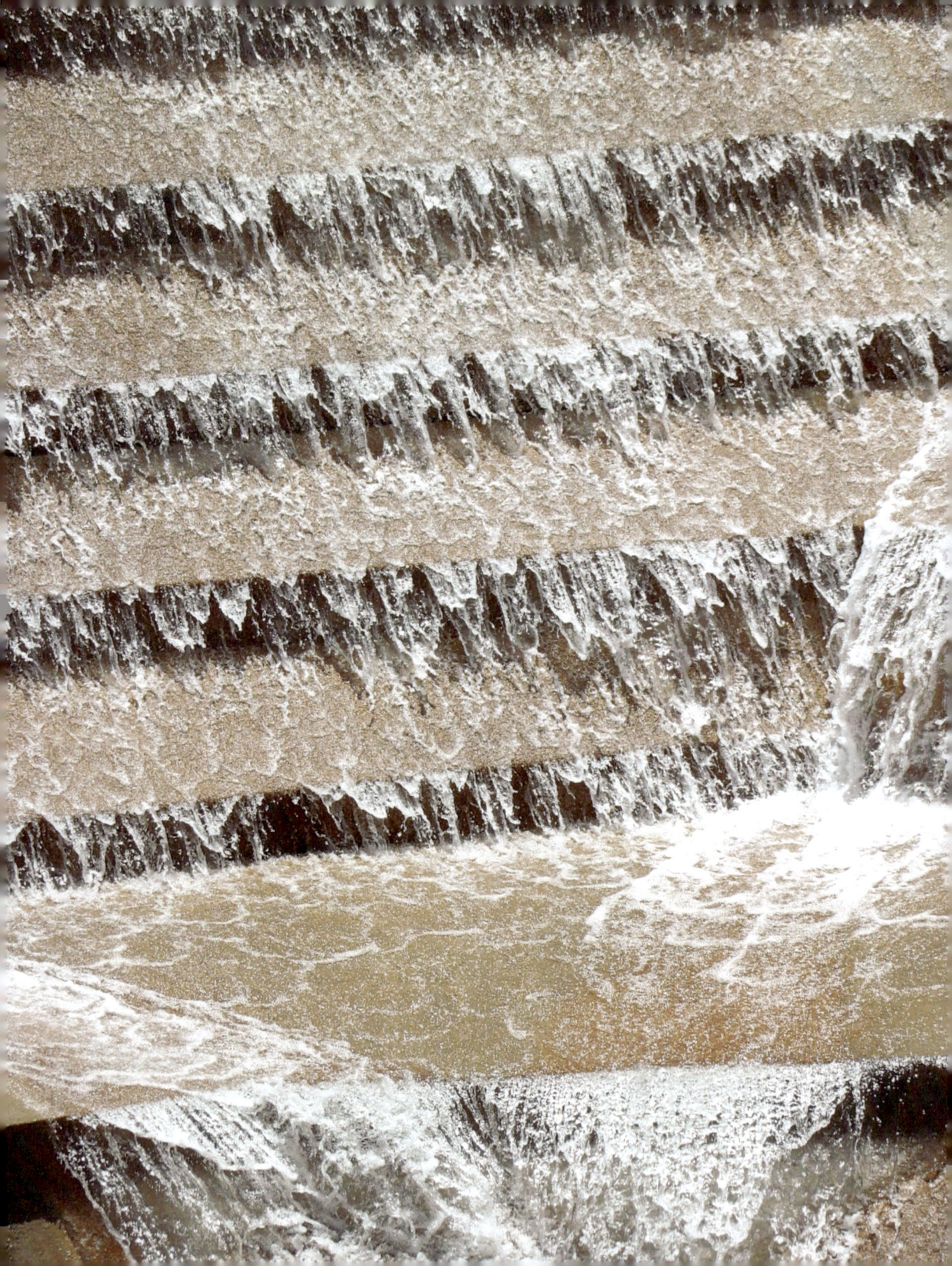

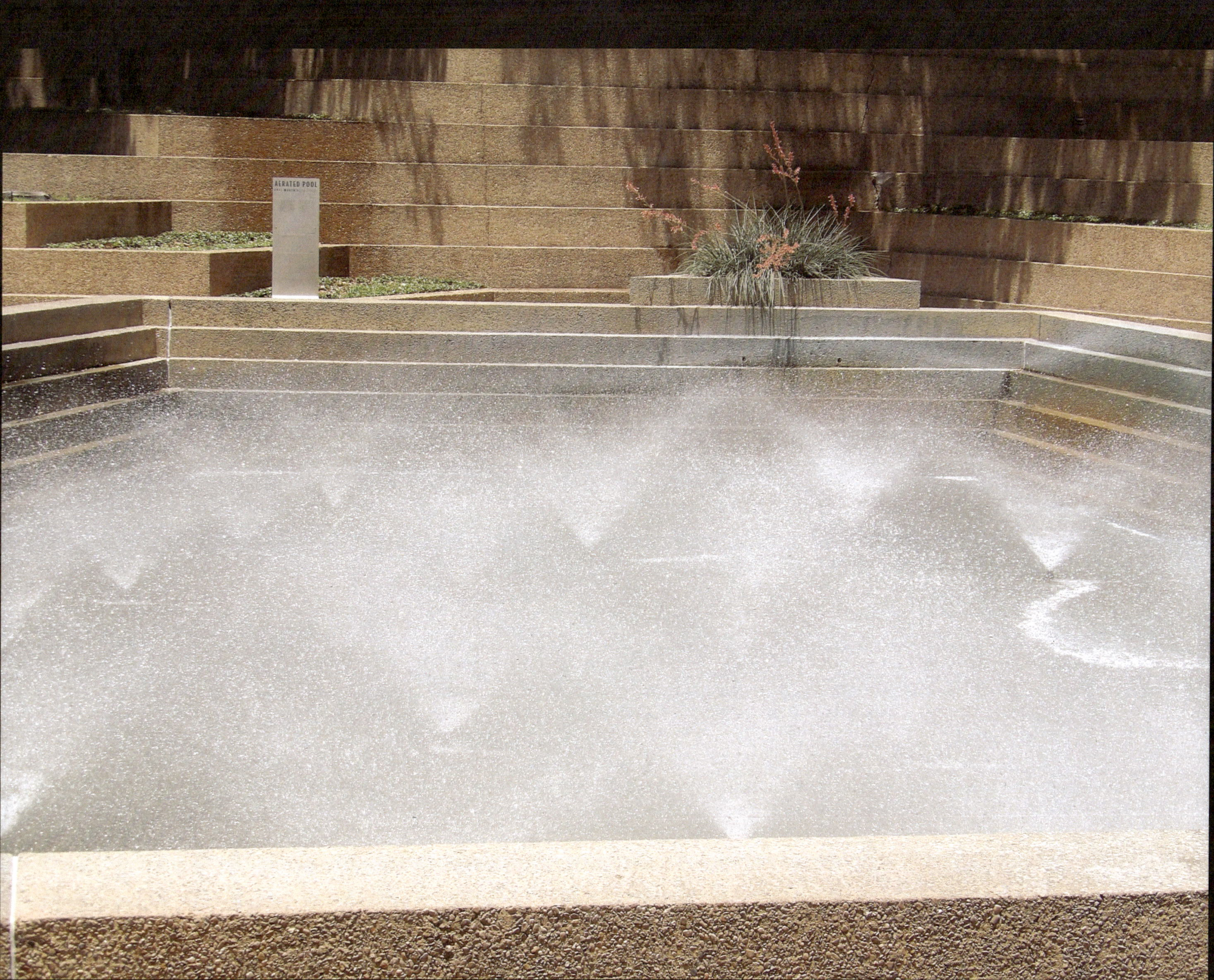
AERATED POOL

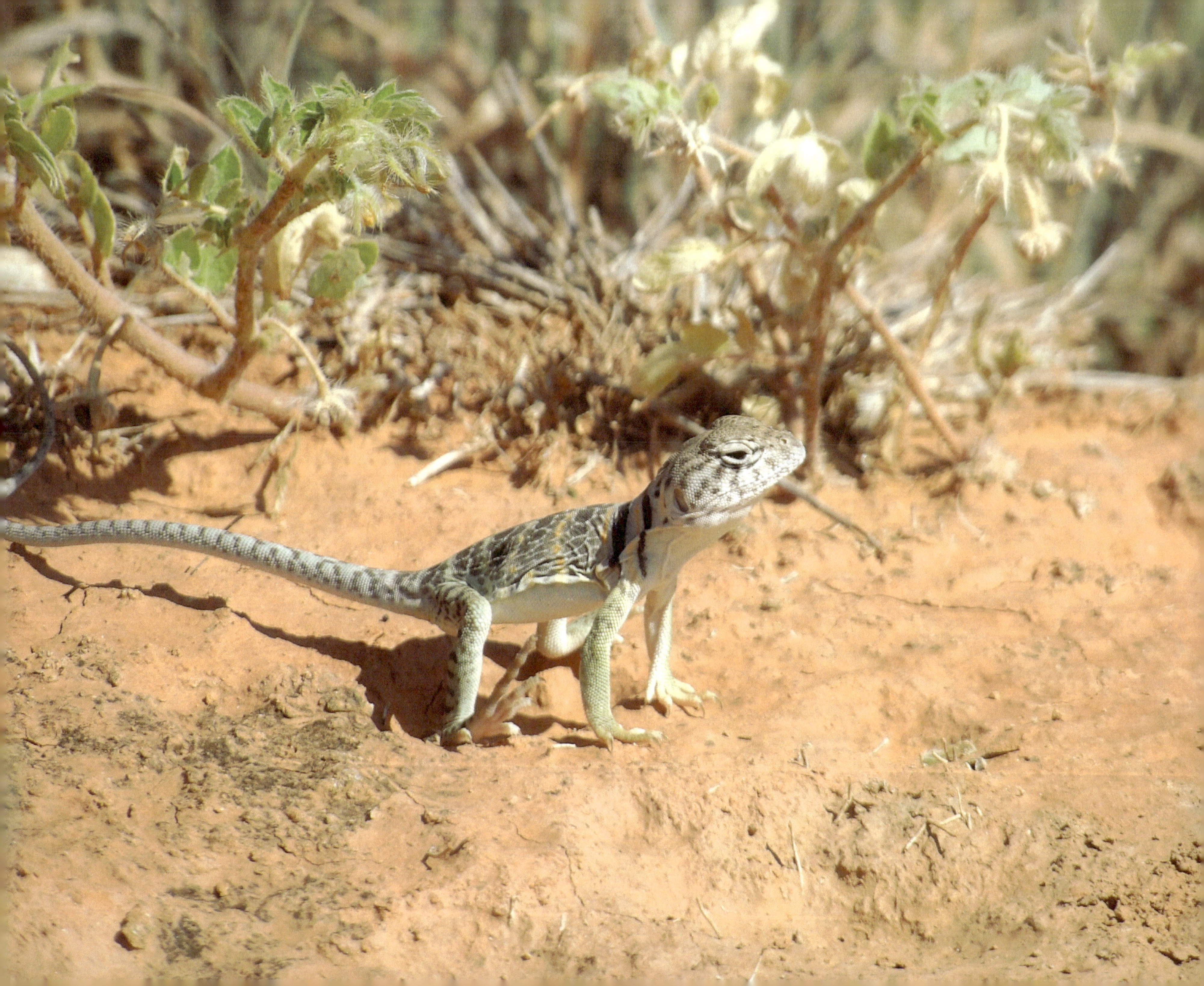

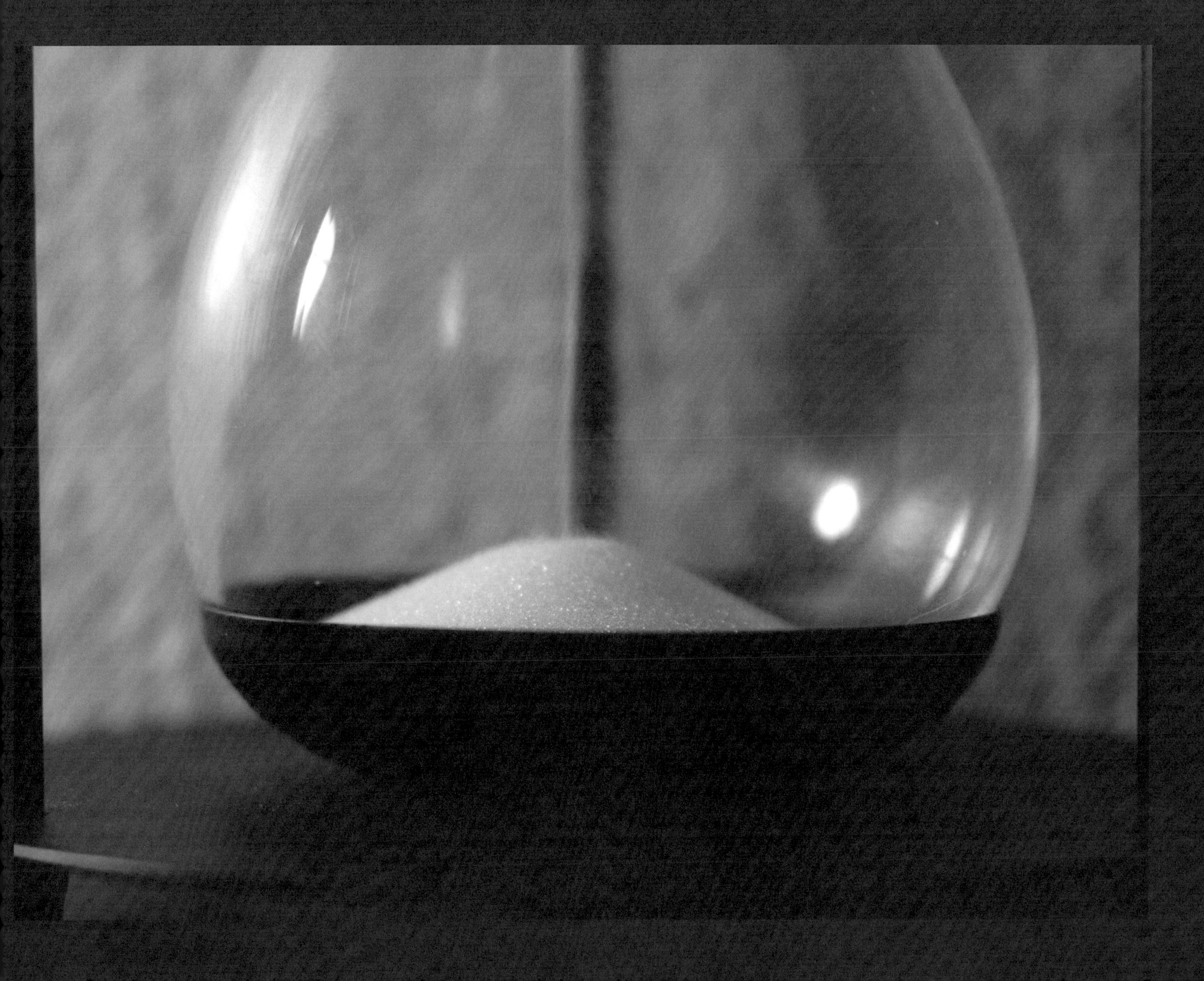

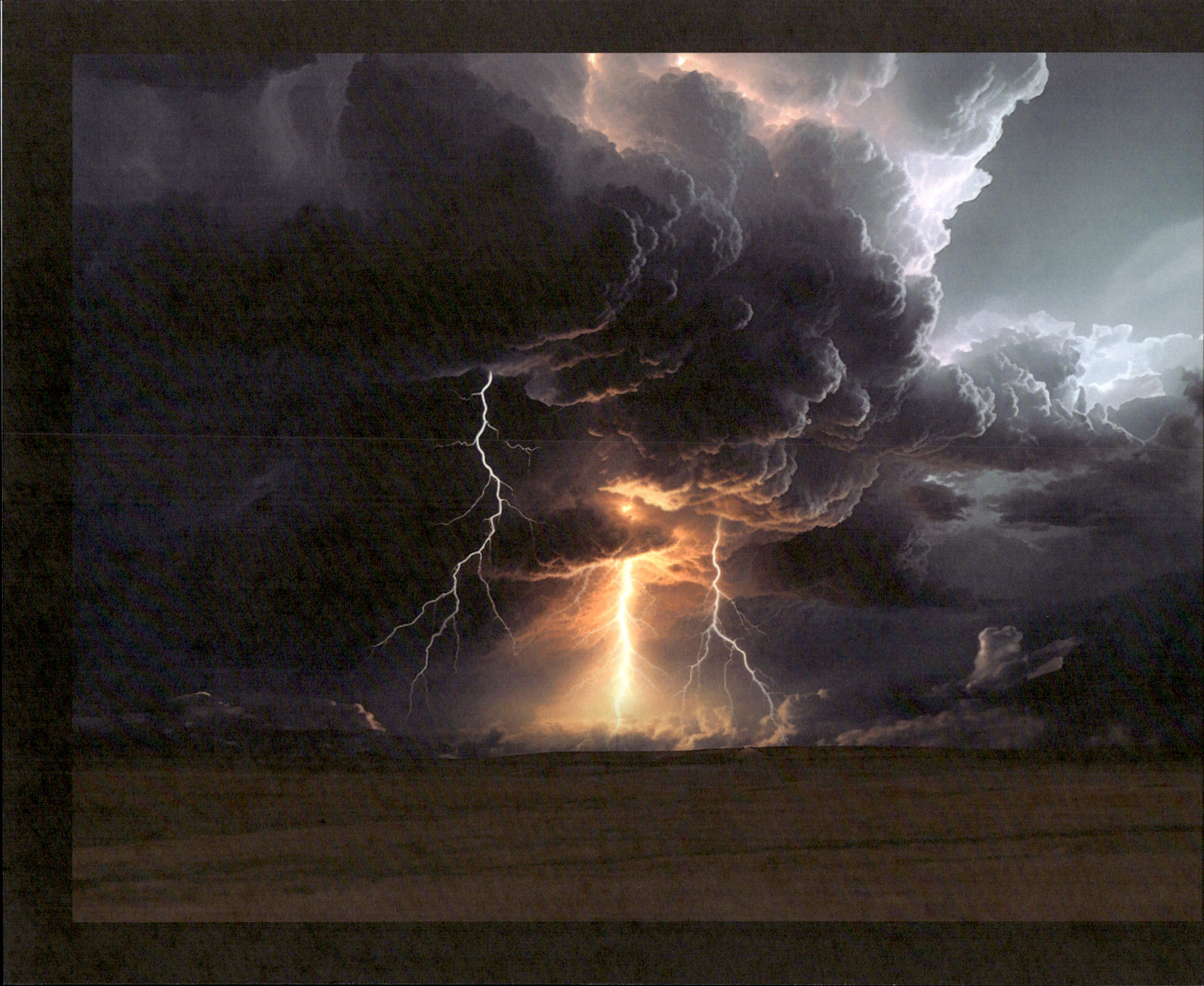

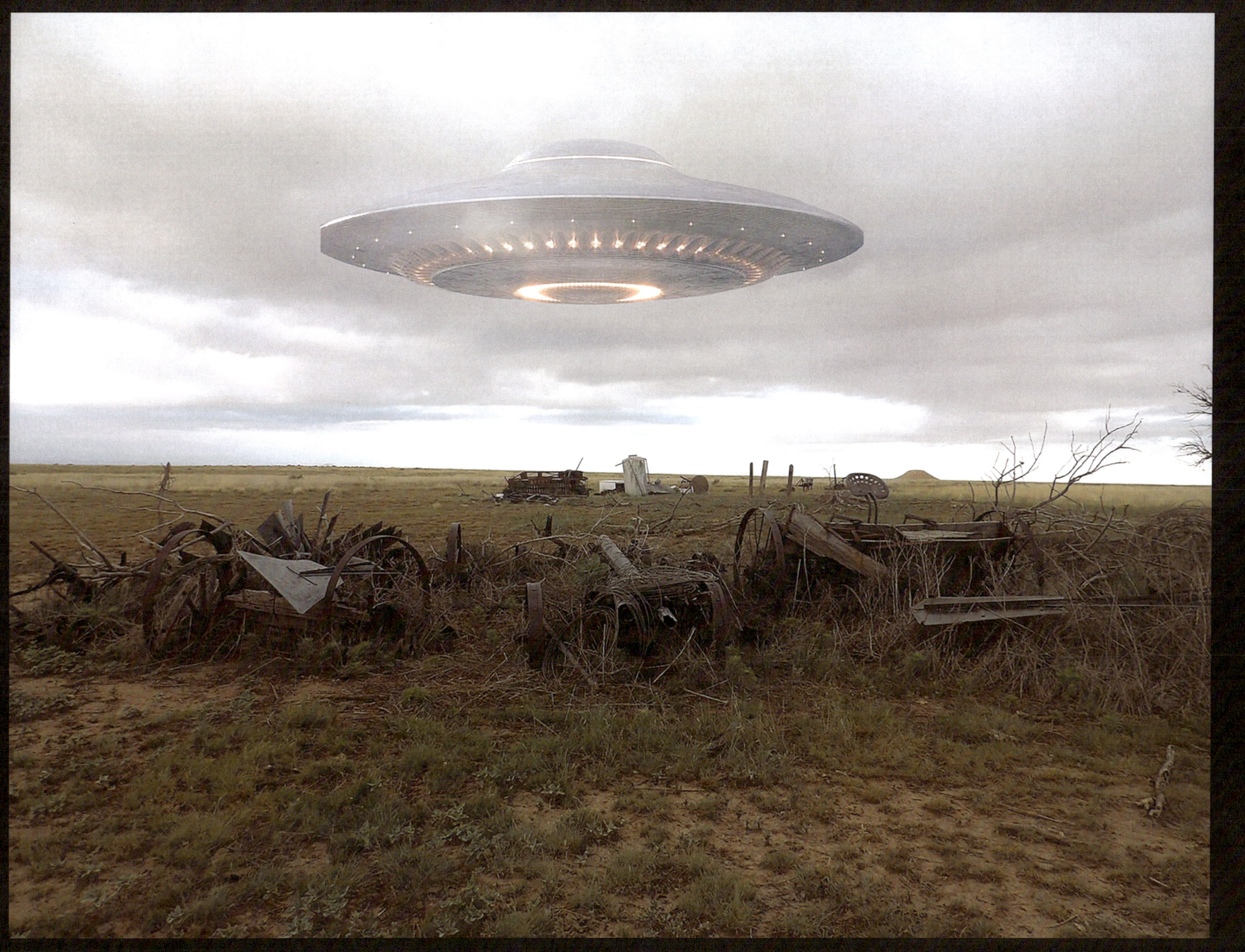

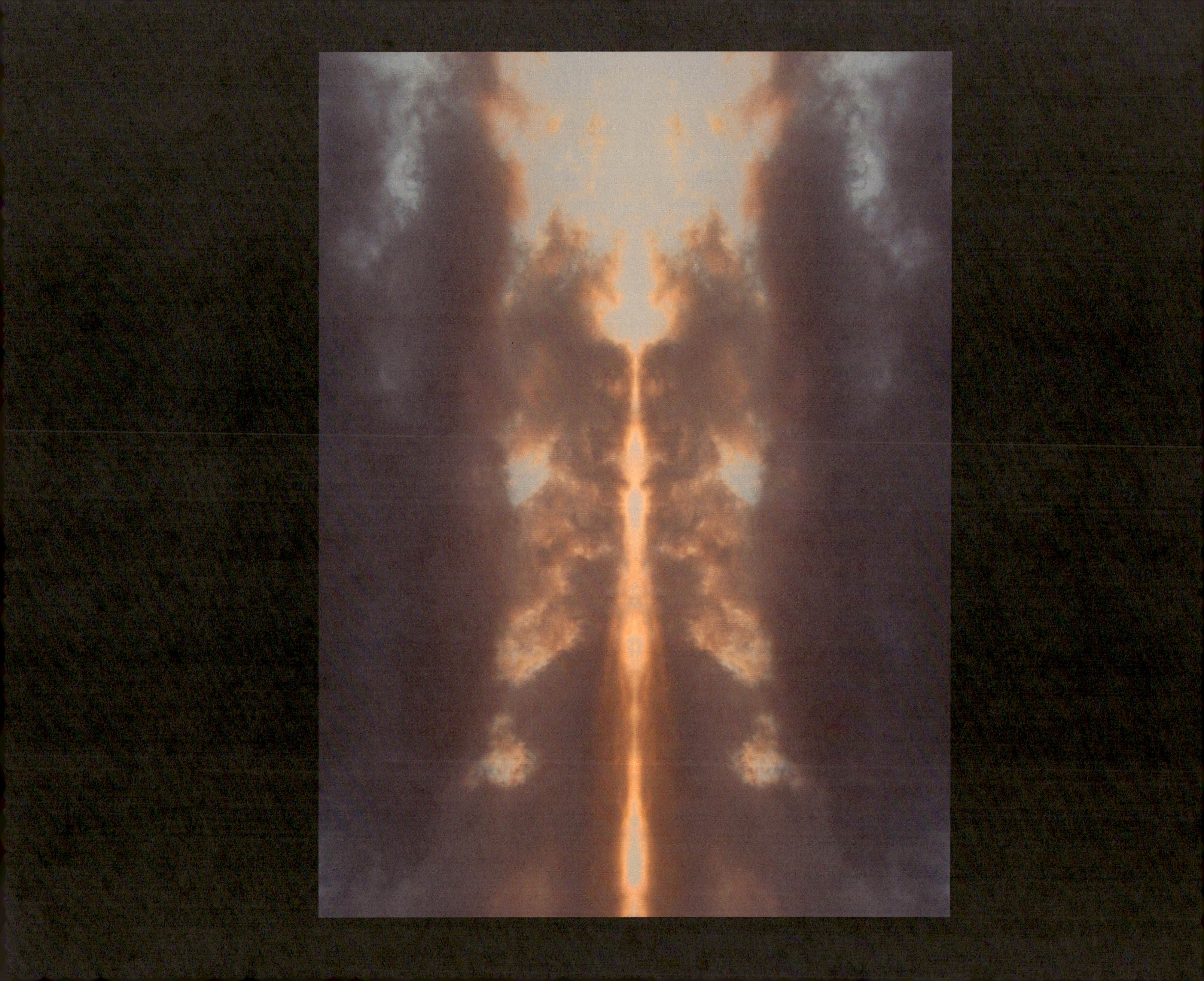

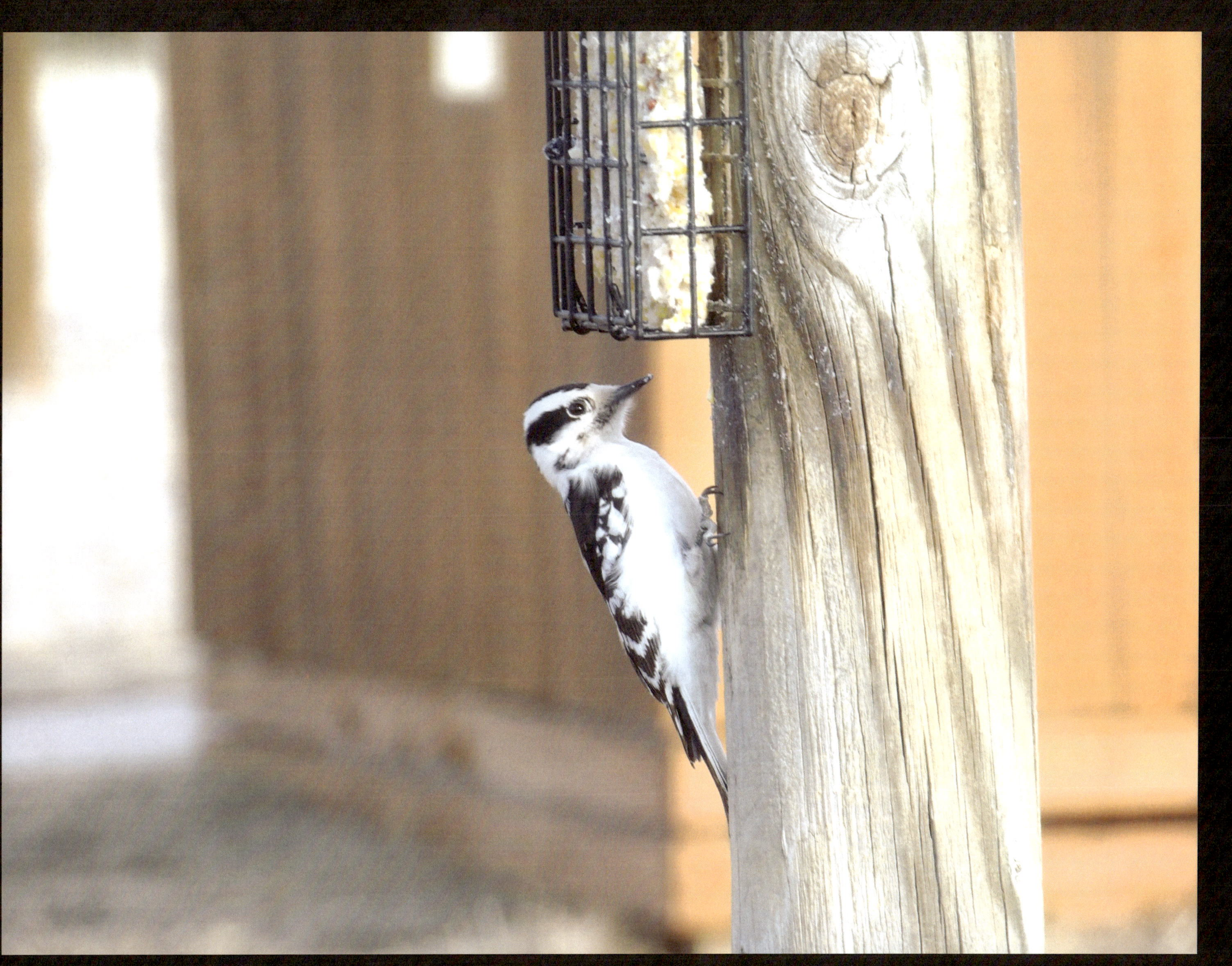

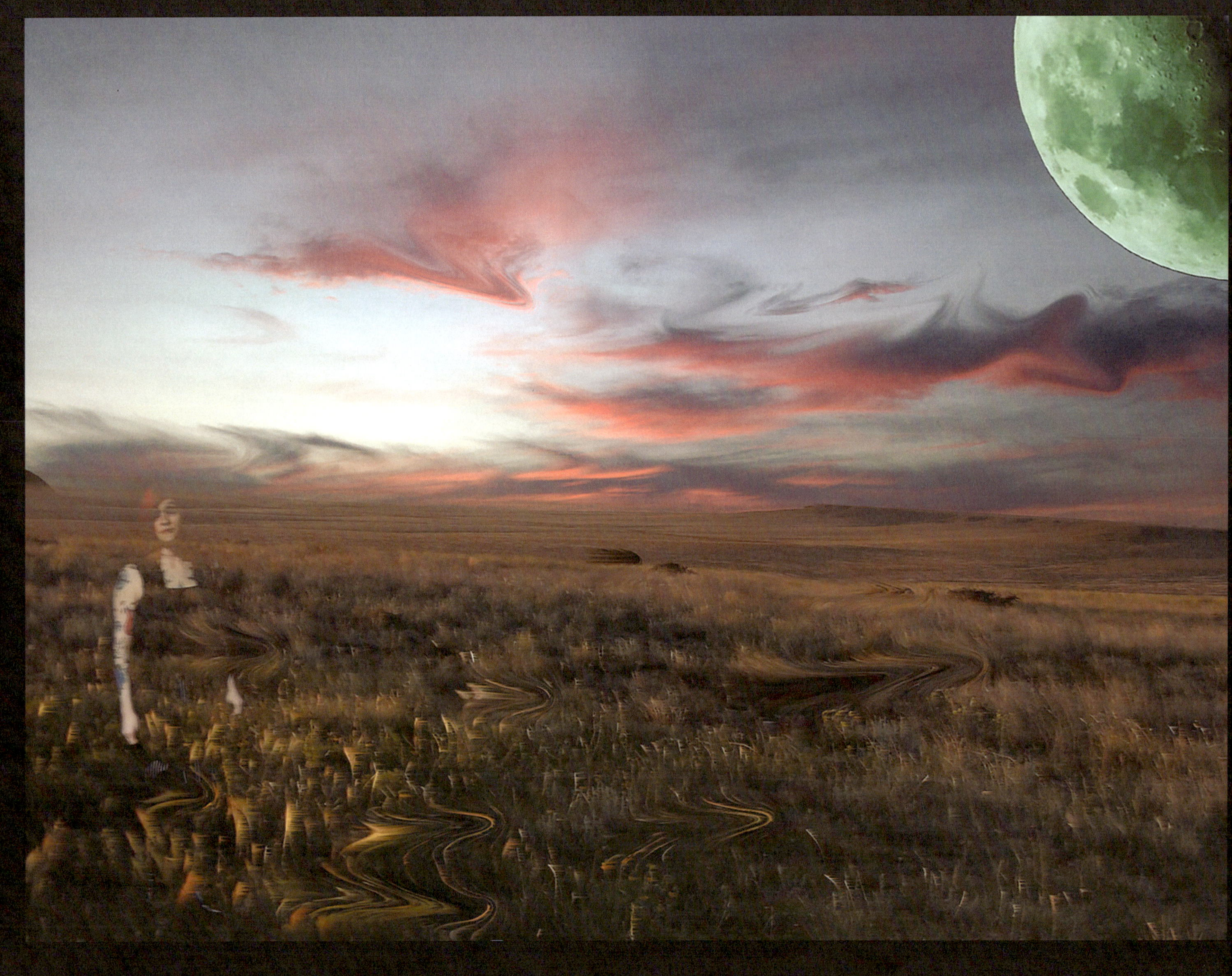

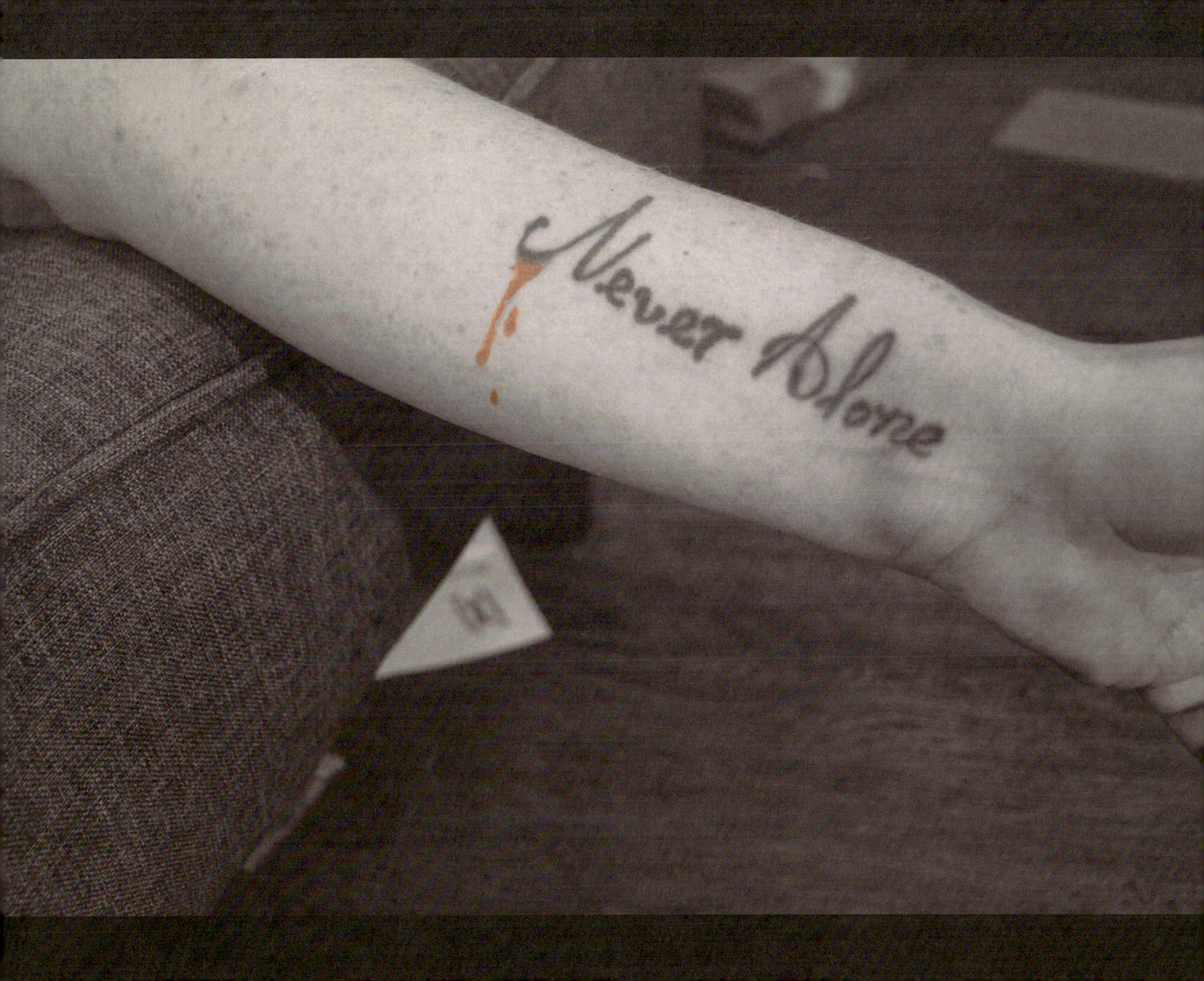

Never Alone

People

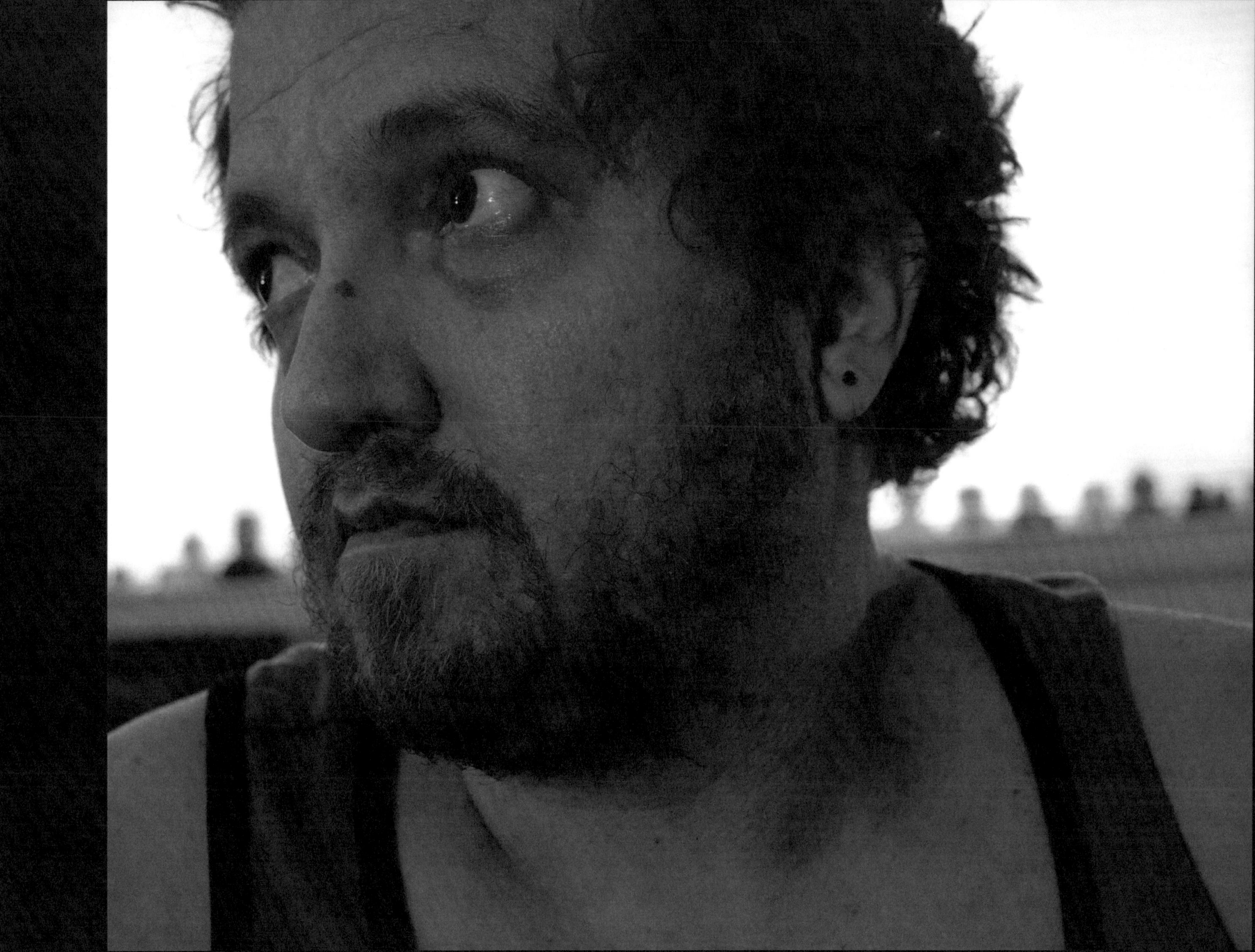

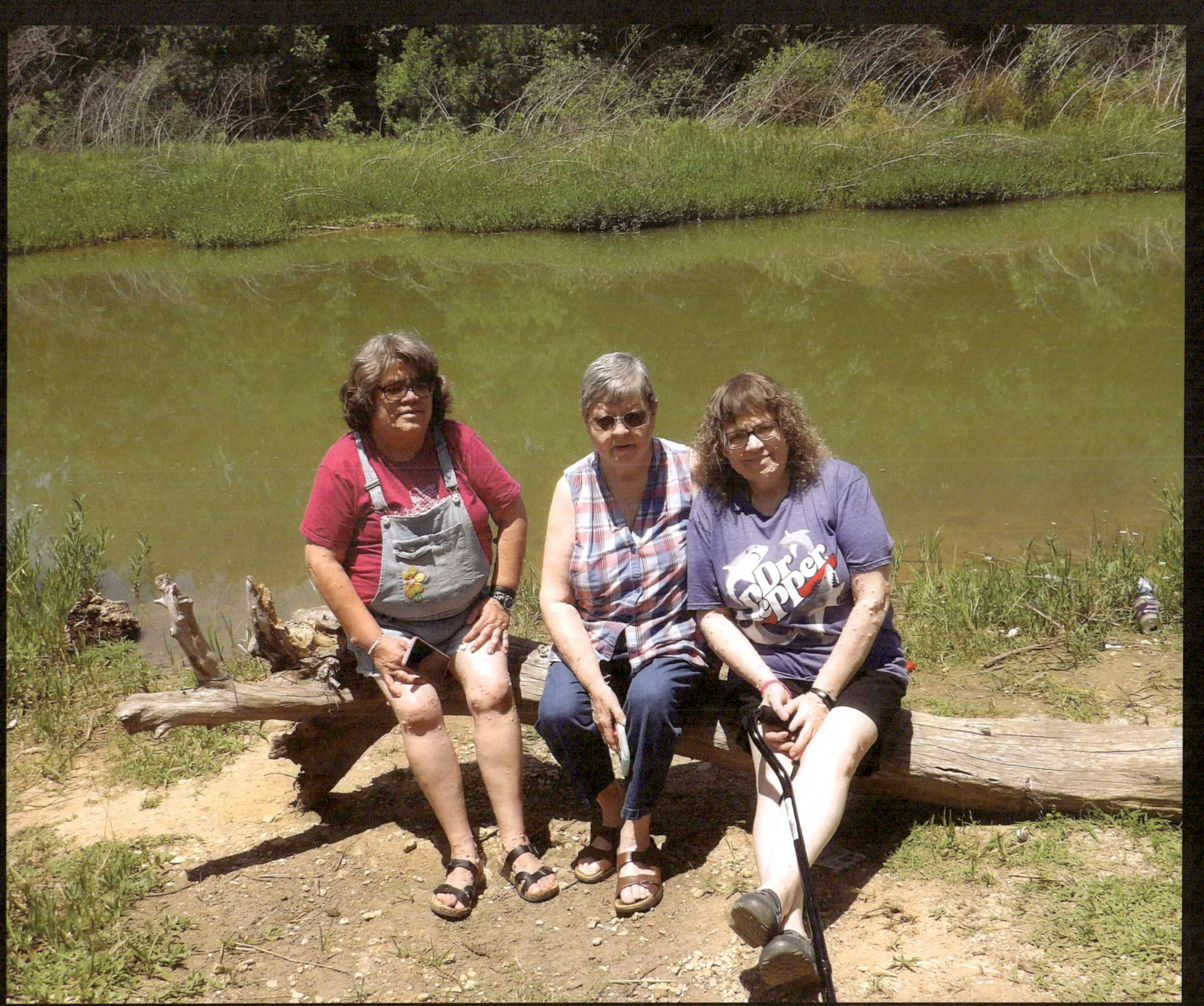

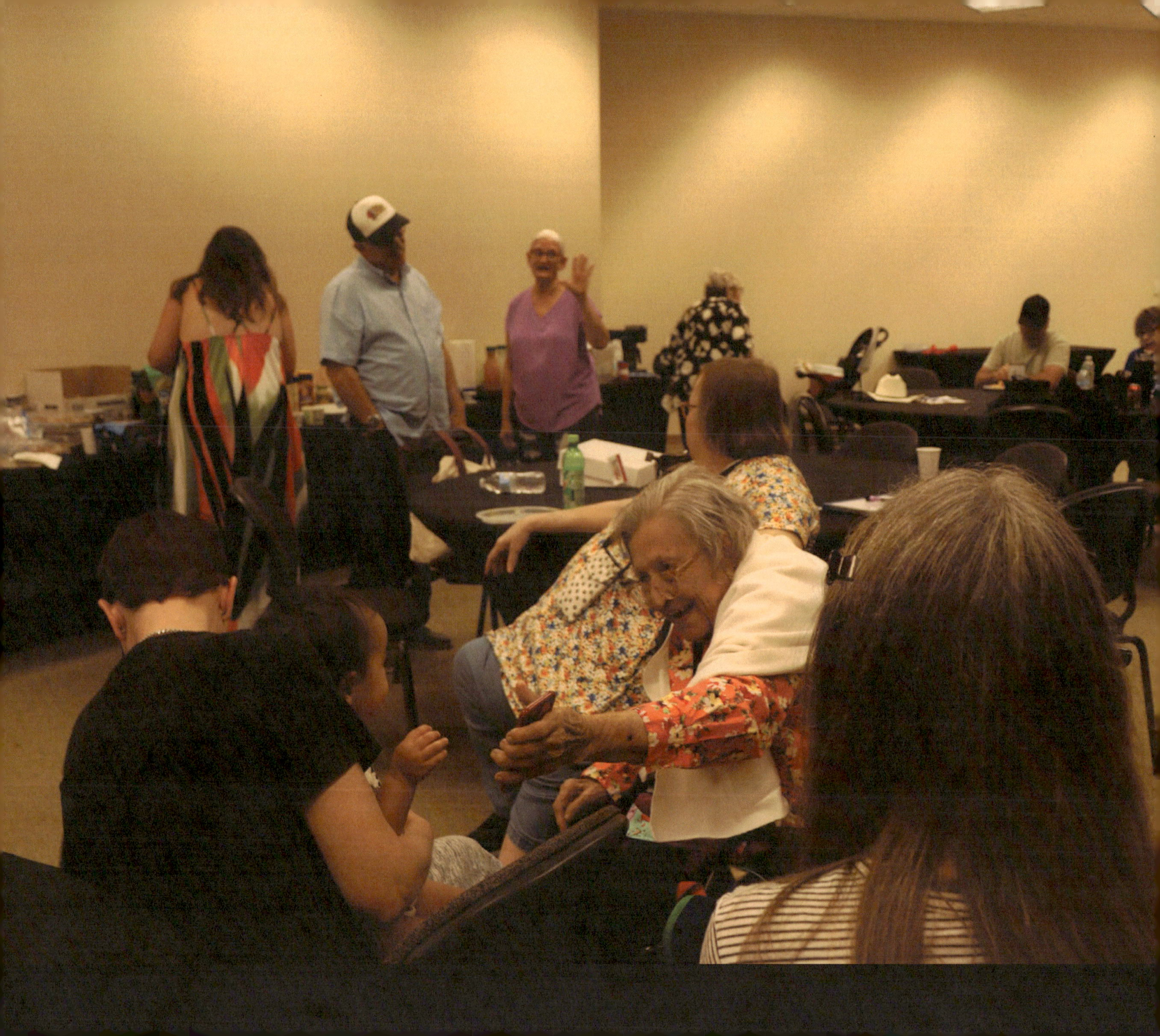

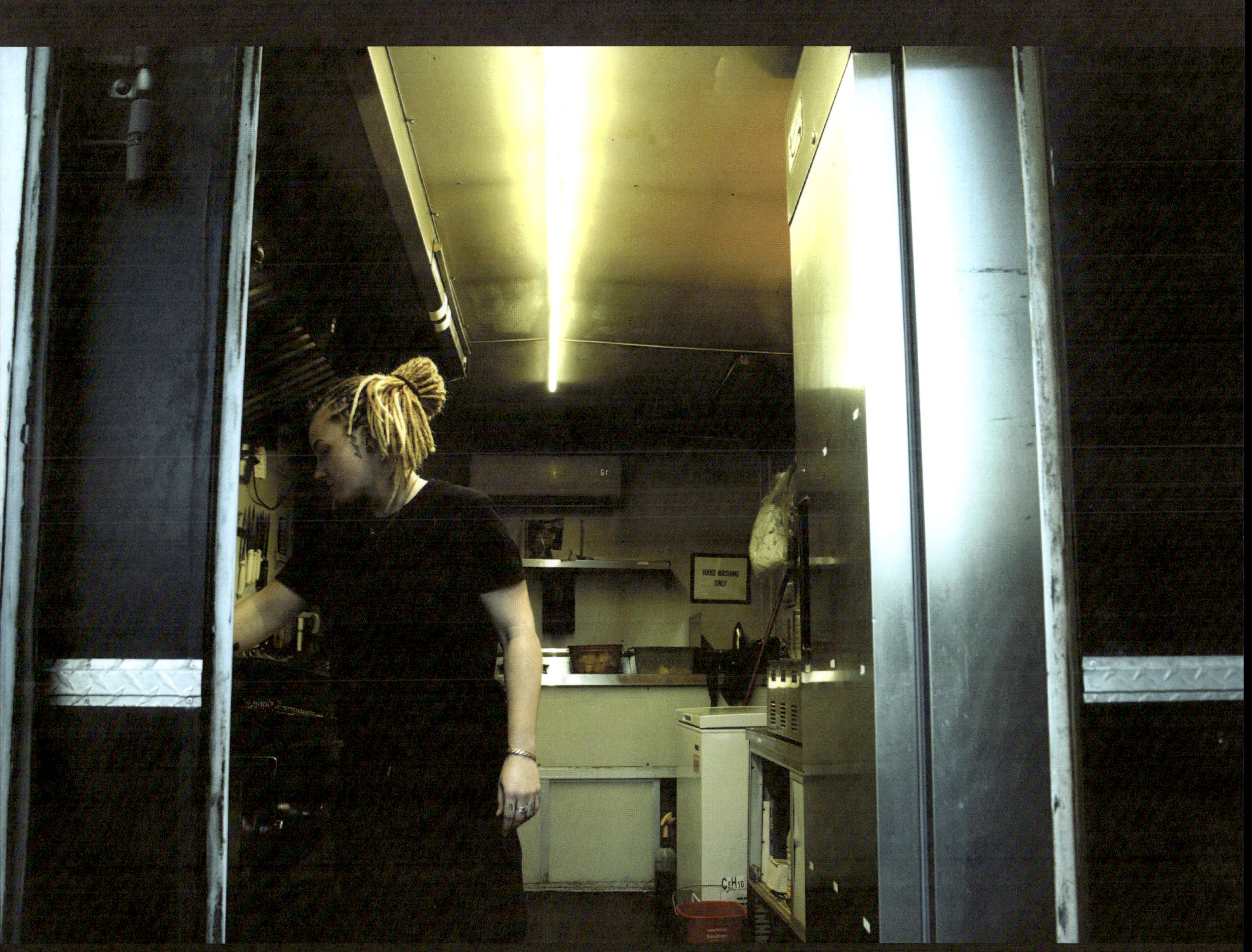

HAND WASHING ONLY
C₅H10

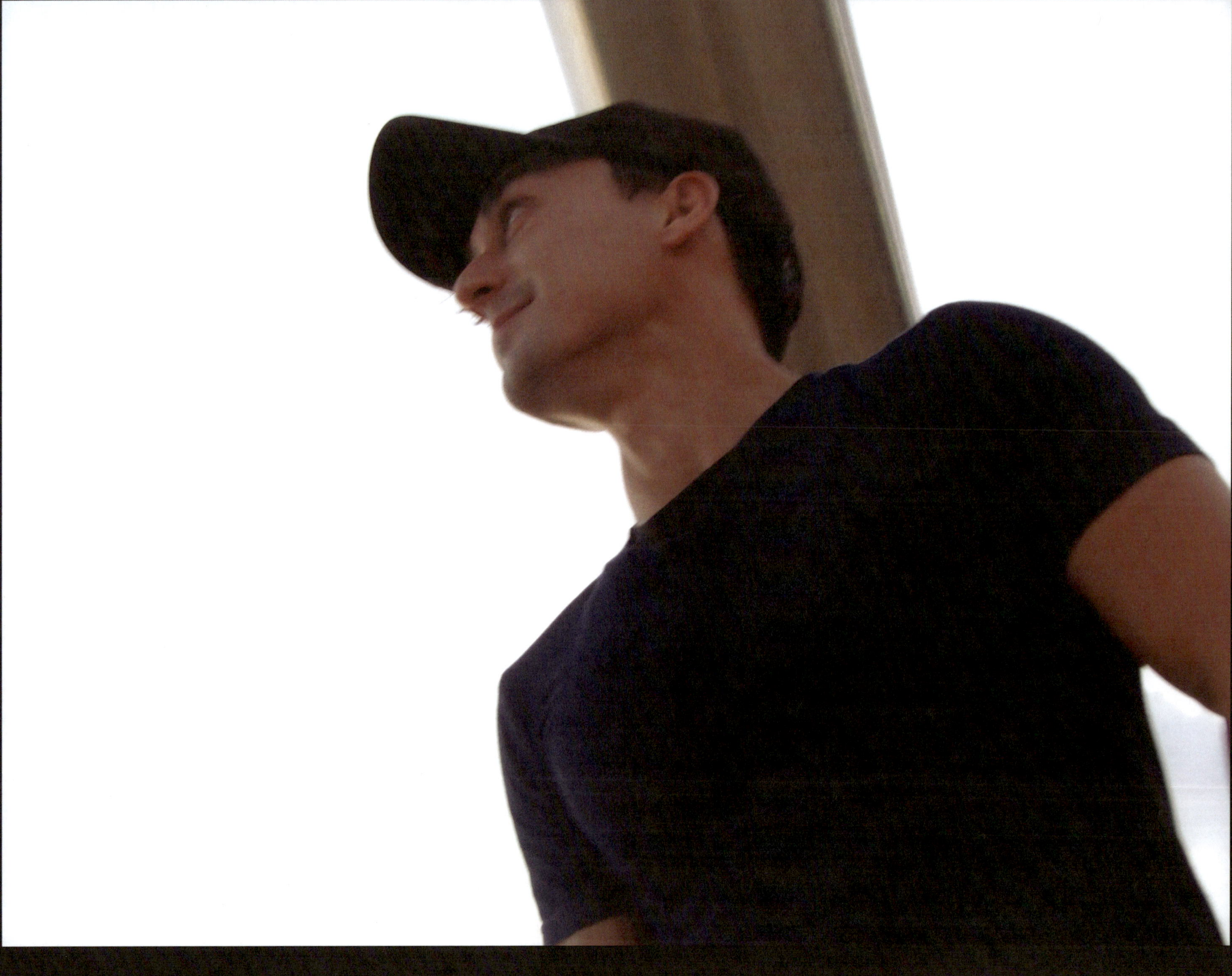

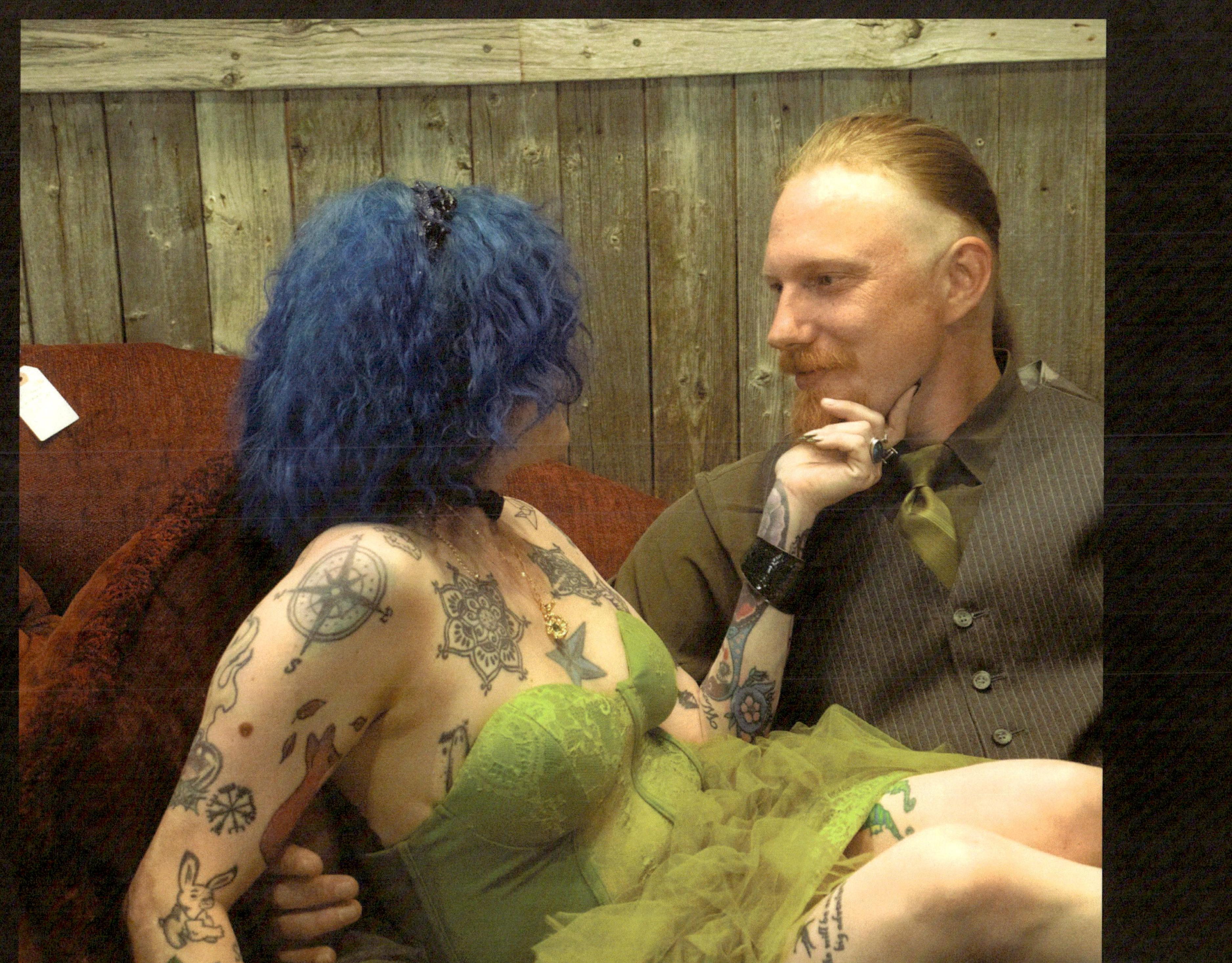

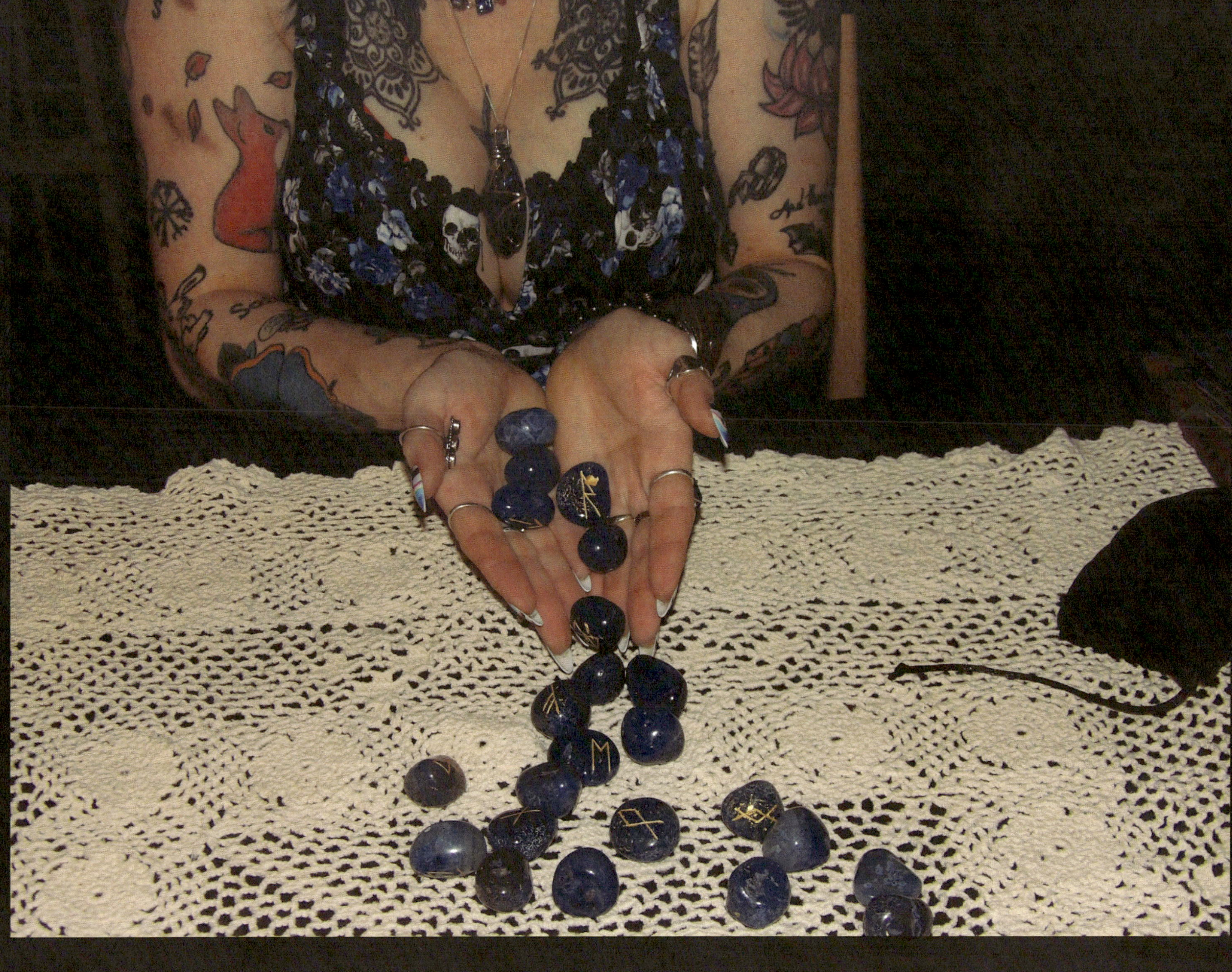

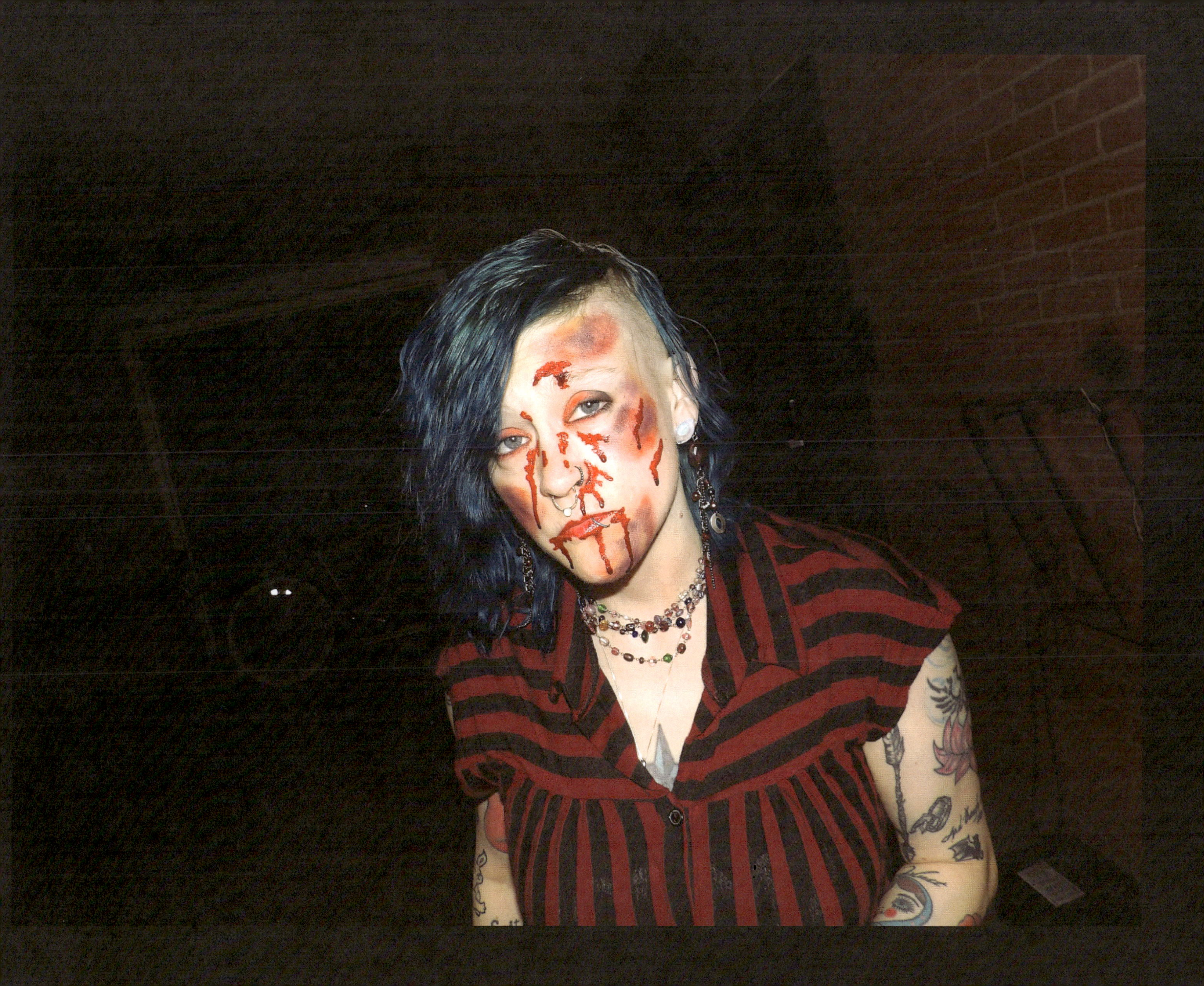

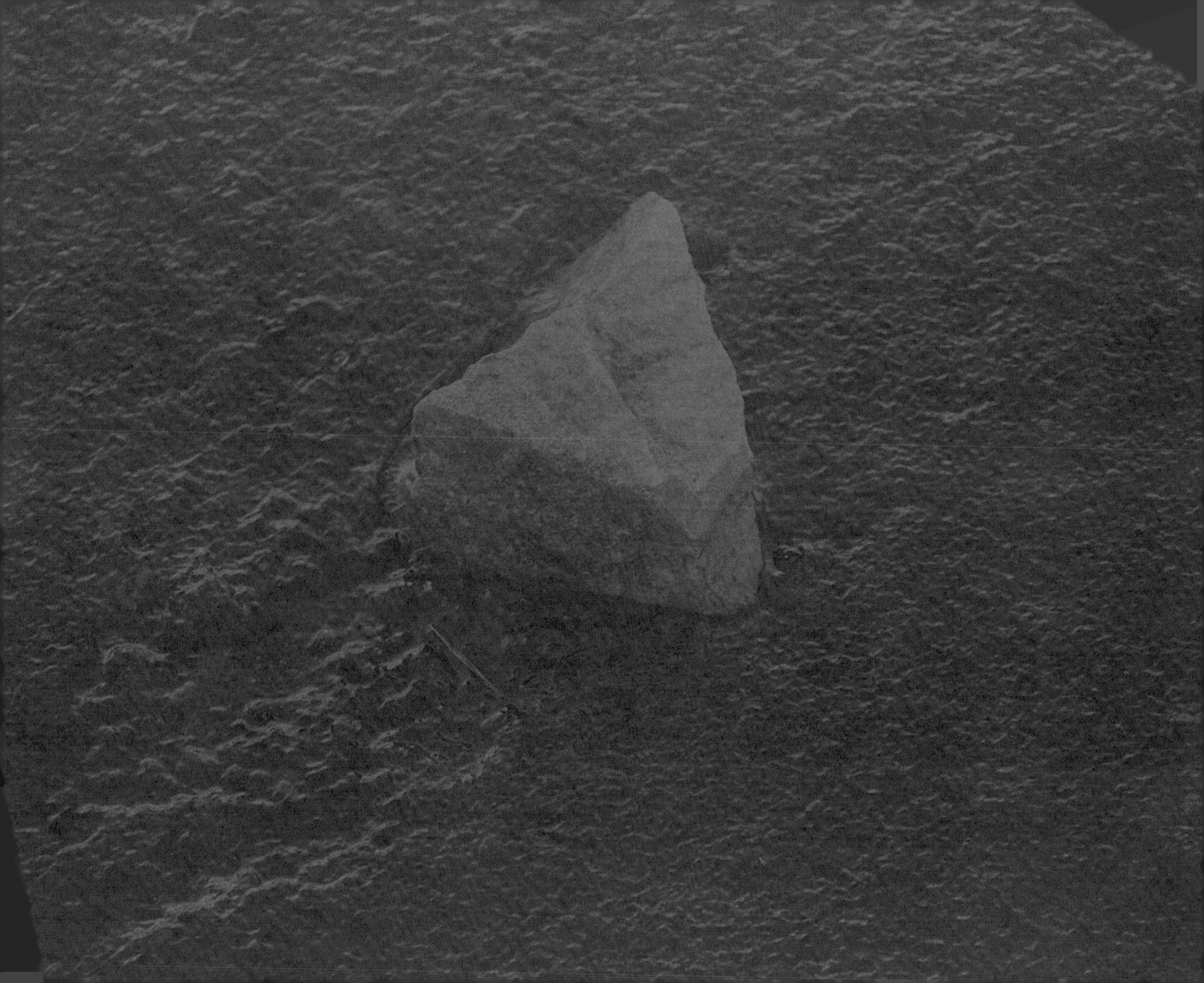

www.ingramcontent.com/pod-product-compliance
Lightning Source LLC
Chambersburg PA
CBRC101241050726
47599CB00012B/1035